Working With The Elderly

A Social Systems Approach

Ellie Brubaker

SAGE PUBLICATIONS
The Publishers of Professional Social Science
Newbury Park   Beverly Hills   London   New Delhi

For information address:

SAGE Publications, Inc.
2111 West Hillcrest Drive
Newbury Park, California 91320

SAGE Publications Inc.
275 South Beverly Drive
Beverly Hills
California 90212

SAGE Publications Ltd.
28 Banner Street
London EC1Y 8QE
England

SAGE PUBLICATIONS India Pvt. Ltd.
M-32 Market
Greater Kailash I
New Delhi 110 048 India

Printed in the United States of America

Library of Congress Cataloging-in-Publication Data

Brubaker, Ellie.
   Working with the elderly.

   Bibliography: p.
   Includes index.
   1. Social work with the aged.   2. Social systems.
I. Title.
HV1451.B78   1987   362.6′042   87-8495
ISBN 0-8039-2589-1
ISBN 0-8039-2590-5   (pbk.)

Contents

This book is dedicated to my parents, Bart and Edith Bartholomew, who approach aging with anticipation and enthusiasm.

Preface

Working with the Elderly: A Social Systems Approach was written to provide information about human service work with older individuals. Human services for the elderly have increased in the past decade. Although literature is available to service providers concerning service delivery to aged clients, little information exists about work with older clients during each stage of the service delivery process.

The primary objective of this book is to provide information, from a social systems perspective, about the values, purpose, knowledge, and tasks necessary to provide human services to elderly clients. Throughout the book, this information is applied to each phase of the service delivery process. Several themes are developed in the book. These include the assumption that successful work with older clients requires attention to clients' environments; an emphasis on application of values, purpose, and knowledge to practice; a focus of the process of work with older clients; and an awareness of the needs that elderly clients experience.

Information within this book is beneficial to upper-level students and graduate students in the human service and gerontology fields, and to human service professionals who provide services to elderly clients. Individuals from various professions, including social work, nursing, counseling, and psychology, can utilize the information presented here.

The contributions and support of a number of individuals facilitated the writing of this book. The social systems orientation held by Ralph Anderson and Irl Carter have obviously influenced the direction of the book. Although their specific contributions are cited throughout the book, their perspective has given impetus to many of the ideas presented here. I am especially grateful for the valuable suggestions provided by Ralph Anderson, John H. Behling, Jordan I. Kosberg, and Joel Leon, who each took the time to extensively review this manuscript. Appreciation is also expressed to Susan Kilbane for proofreading and providing comments on the entire manuscript. This book could not have been written without the support of my family. Tim Brubaker consistently provided encouragement. Laurie and Christie, my daughters, were flexible and helpful throughout the process.

1

INTRODUCTION

Within the past two decades, the proportion of older people in our society has increased significantly. The elderly are viewed as a special population group and monies for the development of programs have been targeted for them. For example, the Older American's Act has encouraged the development of programs and services that support elderly who remain in the community. Long-term care facilities have created programs to better serve older residents and their families. New developments in medicine have resulted in an increased life span and have contributed to the health of individuals in their later years. Also, academic programs have been developed in the field of gerontology, with specific gerontological content being incorporated into graduate social work and interdisciplinary programs. As a result, human services for the elderly have expanded in numerous creative ways.

For human service professionals providing direct services to older individuals and their families, descriptive and research literatures are increasingly available. The practitioner can find many sources that provide descriptive information about older persons and their functioning (for example, Weeks, 1984; Aiken, 1982; Atchley, 1985; Janzen and Harris, 1980). Various scholarly journals provide the practitioner with research information about how elderly people function physically, socially, emotionally, and financially. Specific texts and articles for human service providers outline helpful knowledge and skills for work with the elderly (for example, Steinberg and Carter, 1983; Harbert and Ginsberg, 1979; Lowy, 1979; Beaver, 1983; Weiner et al., 1978). For the most part, knowledge about older clients has focused on issues, content areas, and service settings. However, *a gap in the literature exists for the service provider desiring information and guidance about the various phases of the service delivery process within an environmental context.* Knowledge about the process of delivering service to elderly clients is necessary for successful service provision.

This book is written for service providers who work with elderly clients. Information is provided that examines and describes older persons physically, financially, emotionally, and socially. Knowledge about the elderly is then applied to the service delivery *process.*

The stages a service provider and client go through within a professional relationship may be similar in format to the stages followed in any professional relationship (Brubaker, 1983). However, in content, the stages of a relationship with members of any special population group should be based on the specific needs of that group. For example, a practitioner working with a hostile, abusive parent requires different knowledge and skills than does the practitioner assigned to an elderly widow who is grieving for her spouse. Consequently, in this book, each stage of the service provider-elderly client relationship is integrated with knowledge about the elderly in order to provide the reader with specific information about the process of work with older clients. The information within this book is presented from a social systems perspective. A social systems perspective directs the service provider to examine the various systems with which the client interacts and to acknowledge the relationships that the client has formed in those systems. This perspective is valuable when working with the elderly. Clients of all ages, including older clients, interact with various social systems (both formal and informal), which they are influenced by and which they influence.

FRAMEWORK

Service providers' practice with clients invariably reflects their acknowledged, or unacknowledged, perceptions concerning what service provision involves. Certainly this book represents the author's conception of work with clients. Various models of service provision exist and the author's framework is drawn from a variety of perspectives. This book reflects the belief that service provision involves activities carried out by professionals who adhere to a *value* system, are directed by a *mission* (which derives its structure from the value base), utilize *knowledge* (developed from value, mission, empirical research, and practice wisdom), carry out *tasks* to fulfill the mission, and are *accountable* to sanctioning bodies. This view is illustrated in the Figure 1.1.

The frame of reference presented is directly related to a social systems orientation. The social systems approach mandates that clients' internal and external functioning be recognized, allowing for a consideration of their total makeup, the larger environment, its component parts, and the relationship of all these aspects. For the elderly, attention to their intellectual, psychological, and physical functioning is as necessary as is attention to external systems with which they relate in social, financial, and other ways. The service provider, as a social system with values, purpose, knowledge, and skills, is also an external system that influences the client.

Values. Different professional groups adhere to various value systems that direct their practice. However, commonalities exist across the helping professions. For example, various helping professions stress the worth and dignity of the client. Human service providers from different fields acknowledge the value of meeting existing needs with available resources in society. The values on which this book's service framework rests include the following:

(1) Society has an obligation to provide for the access of individuals to resources that allow society's members to meet their needs and develop their potentials.
(2) These resources should be provided in a way that respects the individual society member.

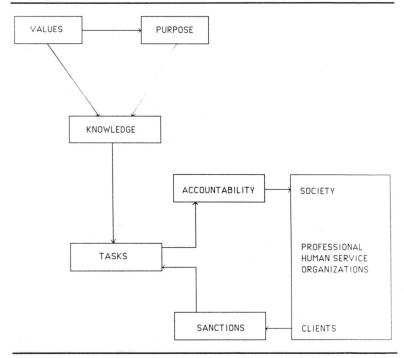

Figure 1.1: Service Provision Framework

(3) Individuals have the responsibility to transact with others in a contributing way.

These values, which are derived from the 1981 "Working Statement on the Purpose of Social Work" (Working Statement, 1981: 6), suggest that individuals require input and resources in order to attain goals. In addition, the dignity and worth of the individual are stressed. Implicitly these values suggest that as individual goals are met, society as a system is freed to seek achievement of its goals. Also implied in the suggestion of society's obligations to individuals is the belief that society can prevent, or contribute to, individual problems by the nature of its transactions with its members. Human service providers, often acting as representatives of society, can directly enhance the individual client's functioning and indirectly enhance society's functioning by adherence to these values.

Attention to values is fundamental. As the building block for all other aspects of professional practice, values motivate and are a common ground on which practitioners stand. Service to the elderly requires a sound value base. In relation to the first value cited above, it is important to believe in the ability of elderly individuals to continue to achieve their potentials. The second value is a reminder that all clients require services to be provided in a manner that enhances their dignity. This may involve showing respect to the clients one serves as well as communicating that respect to other systems involved with the client. For example, the service provider can become a role model for the many agencies and individuals involved with the older client. Research reveals that professionals from many disciplines prefer not to work with older clients (Kosberg and Harris, 1978) and have stereotypic beliefs about the elderly (Keith, 1977). A value that calls for respect of the older client requires a view of each client as an individual and fosters a desire to provide services.

The elderly not only have the responsibility to contribute to society, as the third value suggests, but also the desire and capability. As Chapter 3 will note, older persons reciprocate in relationships in which they are involved and often provide support to family members and other individuals and agencies within their communities. The values of human service practice direct the mission, or purpose, for work with older clients.

Purpose. Human service agencies are social systems that become involved at the point of interaction between individuals and the environment (at the point of transaction) in an attempt to help match resources with need. Therefore, the purpose of the human service worker is focused on encouraging and enhancing transactions between individuals and their environments and on changing transactions that prevent resources from reaching needs. A social systems orientation suggests that if a change in transactions between individuals and their environments is effected, a change in both the individuals and their environments will also occur. Social work is an example of a profession that seeks to match individuals and society for the purpose of enhancing individual coping skills as well as increasing the environment's ability to support individual growth (Gordon, 1969).

Human service workers should strive to increase the ability of the environment to provide resources in a way that does not contribute to the development of individual problems but rather that seeks to prevent and alleviate those problems. In this role, the service provider may act as an advocate for the older client, representing the client's needs to appropriate agencies and significant others. In addition, it is necessary for service providers to deal with individuals who are already experiencing problems. This, in turn, facilitates their ability to cope in relation to their environments.

This perspective has historical support in the human services. For example, social work has long recognized the necessity for looking beyond the individual to the environment for solutions to difficulties individuals experience. The 1958 working definition of social work (Working Definition, 1958) acknowledged the relationship between society and the individual and the need for social work, as a helping profession, to have an impact on this relationship. Gordon (1969) proposed the above view of social work. Schwartz (1969) emphasized the need to aid individuals and the suprasystem in maintaining balance. Others have stressed the value of matching individuals and society (Klein, 1972), while Germain (1973) emphasized the importance of an ecological perspective that attends to the "adaptative" fit of individuals and their environments. More recently, Hartman (1981) suggested that professionals go beyond the individual, both in thought and in practice, to acknowledge and utilize the resource of the family. Brill (1985) relied on the social systems approach in her development of a helping model and outlined various advantages of that approach for direct service to clients. The advantages of looking to both the individual and the environment include the following: (1) "assuring a unified view of the interlocking components"; (2) allowing the helper to examine how relationships "within the systems . . . will be affected by change within any part of the whole; (3) pinpointing the crucial point here determining type and mode of intervention to be utilized; (4) anticipating probable results of intervention at each level" (Brill, 1985: 62).

The human service worker involved with older clients is in a position to facilitate matching between the client and the larger environment. Most older persons are not isolated (Shanas, 1979b), and their interactions with others in society are many and varied. The character of these interactions can either exacerbate or ameliorate the problems of the elderly. It is at the point of interaction that the service provider can best match resources to client need. For those clients who are isolated, the provider can function as an advocate and/or liaison in the initiation of relationships between the elderly client and the larger society. These activities on the service provider's part require knowledge of the elderly and their interactions with others. In addition, knowledge about society's response to older individuals is a requisite.

Knowledge. The development and use of knowledge in human service work with older clients are necessary. Both empirical research and practical wisdom contribute to the development of a knowledge base for human service workers. The type of knowledge sought should be directed by the values and mission of service providers. However, it is important that values are not substituted for knowledge. Bartlett (1970) has differentiated between knowledge and values, defining values as the desire professionals have for the good of people and knowledge as what is known concerning people. Benefits accrue when humanism and science are blended (Germain, 1973). Maintaining a strong value orientation while utilizing a body of knowledge will enhance the effectiveness of service and increase credibility with clients and society.

As noted, specialized knowledge of the client group to be served is vital. A lack of knowledge about the elderly can hinder the practitioner in assessing client need (Brubaker, 1984), resource availability, and the matching of the two. For example, an older client may mention to a service provider that she is unable to complete small tasks around her home. If the provider lacks knowledge about the helping relationships that exist between the majority of older clients and their families, she may arrange for the client to receive homemaker services without inquiring about the help the client's family gives or desires to give. Family members could respond by decreasing the help they already give to their elderly member with the result that the older client becomes more isolated from relatives than before "help" was provided. Conversely, knowledge about the older client's informal support systems can allow for a blending of informal and formal services to the client (Brubaker and Brubaker, 1984), lessening the possibility of duplication of, or gaps in, service. Knowledge, in combination with values and purpose, can be applied to the tasks of the human service worker.

Task. The task performance of human service workers is related to values, purpose, and knowledge. It follows that the task of service provision is to

(1) facilitate the development and maintenance of linkages between individuals and society (Minahan and Pincus, 1977), and
(2) enhance the matching of resources to need, of both society and individuals.

Service providers, in carrying out these tasks, must be armed with a general knowledge base and have developed specialized knowledge and skills.

Human service workers' tasks with older clients flow from values, mission, and knowledge, as do tasks with any population. Throughout this book, specific tasks carried out in service provision with the elderly are discussed in relation to the service provision process. Process is central to carrying out tasks. Use of process allows service provision to be planned and structured, calling for the service provider to attend to knowledge, values, and mission while applying skill to various situations.

Accountability and sanction. Service providers are accountable to various sanctioning bodies. In providing service to the elderly, professionals are first accountable to their older clients. This accountability often extends to the social support system of those clients. Service providers may be as involved with both formal and informal support systems as they are with their older clients. In addition, agencies within the aging network (e.g., area councils on aging) and others within the larger society have expectations of the human service worker's practice. Finally, practitioners are accountable to their professional organizations, which establish expectations for practice. Accountability must exist in terms of both process and outcome. As professionals, we take responsibility, along with the client and the society, for the effectiveness of our work. This is not to imply a belief that we alone are responsible for the outcome of our involvement with clients, but rather to suggest that if service providers have had input into outcome, some evidence of that should exist. Through accountability, professionals seek sanction for practice from clients, society and the professional bodies to which they belong.

PLAN FOR THE BOOK

This book integrates the model of service provision, described above, with the process of work with older clients. Chapters 2 and 3 provide background information about the social systems approach and the elderly population. Chapter 2 describes the social systems approach. This approach is a relevant paradigm from which to examine direct service to elderly clients. A social systems approach allows the provider to focus on the older client, while preventing neglect of the intervening aspects of the client's environment, aspects that influence and are influenced by the client's behavior. The chapters that follow refer to the social systems approach in presenting a framework for direct service provision to older clients.

Background information about the elderly is provided in Chapter 3. Knowledge about the relationships between older persons and the social systems with which they interact is necessary to effective service provision. Just as the elderly are part of larger systems, social and economic, older persons are also systems in their own right, with physical and emotional subsystems acting and interacting to impact on external relationships. Many readers are knowledgeable about older clients. However, it is helpful to equalize knowledge of readers by providing information about theory and research concerning the elderly and the many arenas in which they function.

Chapters 4 through 8 present information about the service delivery process with older clients. Service provision is a process in which client and provider work together toward matching client need with appropriate resources. The caseworker and older client go through stages of a process similar to that of caseworkers and clients of various age groups. However, within each stage the work differs according to the client's place in the life cycle. Individuals have different needs at different times in their lives and the manner in which those needs are approached and dealt with differs accordingly. These chapters present case material that is analyzed according to the stage of the service provision process it presents, from a social systems perspective.

The initial relationship between service provider and older client is the focus of Chapter 4. Aspects of a professional relationship with older clients are discussed. An emphasis is placed on (1) the importance of beginning the initial relationship with knowledge about older individuals in general, as well as an awareness that each older person is unique; (2) the examination of client's expectations and the explanation of the service provider's role; and (3) ways in which a trusting relationship can be established with older clients.

The data gathering process involved in working with older clients is detailed in Chapter 5. When gaining information about older clients' functioning and needs, the service provider benefits from gaining an awareness of the client's relationships to others. A data gathering format is presented that examines the systems with which the older client interacts, as well as the way the older client secures and expends energy in relation to those systems. This chapter presents a case example of a data gathering interview followed by an analysis.

Chapter 6 describes the process of working with clients to set goals for the actual delivery of services. This chapter examines the knowledge that the worker has about client need and aspects of designing a plan for matching resources to need. Attention is given to utilizing the client's social network in this phase of the service delivery process.

The actual service delivery process is presented in Chapter 7. This chapter presents information about strategies for case management in direct service with older clients. Specifically, coordination of services from a social systems perspective is delineated, with an emphasis on utilizing coordination to match resources to need. Information is also provided about education of elderly clients and their social systems. Education is an important aspect in the service delivery process because of its ability to prevent difficulties for older clients and their families. Family life education for the elderly and their significant others is discussed as well as education of social service and other appropriate systems. Case examples and analyses are presented throughout the chapter.

The evaluation and termination phase of the service delivery process is discussed in Chapter 8. This chapter provides a format for evaluating the service delivery endeavor, discusses the role of the client, worker, and client's significant others in the evaluation process, and deals with the direction to be taken when evaluation reveals negative results. The discussion of termination emphasizes (1) the relationship between client, worker, and other involved social systems; (2) helping clients to view their experience as successful, if appropriate; and (3) enhancing clients' future functioning through preparing the client and significant others for problem solving after the service delivery process has ended.

As noted, Chapters 4 through 8 provide information about the process of delivering services to elderly clients. Because a variety of human service professions (for example, nurses, social workers, physicians, homemaker/home health aides) can utilize the framework presented, information about specific professions, agencies, categories of clients or types of problems that clients experience are presented in case examples. To become more specific within the text would narrow the utility of the book.

Chapter 9 discusses future directions for service to the elderly. Present service delivery to the elderly is often hampered by cutbacks in funding and programs, lack of coordination of services, and unaccountability. Effective service delivery requires creativity in response to depleted services. Chapter 9 outlines potential roles for professionals serving elderly clients. This chapter also describes advocacy for direct services to older clients in an era of shrinking monies for service delivery. Finally, the ability of direct service workers to contribute to research and theory about successful service delivery strategies with older clients is discussed.

2

THE SOCIAL SYSTEMS APPROACH

Most service providers have become aware of the fact that the majority of older individuals have developed and maintained social networks. Gerontological literature has provided information about the social supports available to and utilized by the elderly (Shanas, 1979b; Atchley, 1985; Gelfand, 1984). Although service providers are aware that most older people have helping relationships with family and friends, they may relate to clients as individuals separate from their social networks (Blenkner, 1965; Shanas, 1979a; Miller, 1981). There are several reasons why this may occur.

First, service providers may assume that their clientele is different from the majority of the elderly. The clients seen by service providers are often the frail or dependent elderly. These individuals, because of their vulnerability, may require more services than family and friends can provide. In addition, some older clients are among the minority of elderly who lack social support systems. It is because of the type of work human service workers do that they are more likely to come across the elderly client who lacks social supports. However, it is imperative to keep in mind that the majority of older clients are likely to have at least a small support network intact.

Second, knowledge of clients' networks is not always applied to practice. Brill (1985) has stated that helping professionals have traditionally been oriented toward working primarily with the individual as opposed to involving the larger network. Hartman (1981) suggested that the family has too long been ignored in work with clients. This may occur because work with an individual client can appear to be more efficient. Involving others in the service provision process may require more time devoted to goal setting and coordinating individuals and resources. However, ignoring significant others will not prevent them from influencing the service provision process. Rather, their unacknowledged involvement may obstruct planned work with older clients. Supportive others whom service providers have not included may resent the provider's presence and interfere with the work they are performing. Those individuals who are not included may unknowingly work at cross purposes, undoing the work planned with the client. This is exemplified by a study in which families of elderly individuals receiving homecare were not consulted by service providers. "In 19% of the cases mentioned, this [lack of consultation and coordination with family members] resulted in disruptive family influences upon the homecare plan" (Friedman and Kaye, 1980: 119).

If professionals are to have success in matching resources to need, acknowledging the client's total environment is mandated. For example, it will be necessary to question how the older person is currently having needs met and how the professional's involvement will influence the existing support relationship. The support networks of some older individuals are broad. The service provider's involvement with an older client will have repercussions on that individual's total network and the network will influence the provision of services.

As noted in Chapter 1, the social systems approach expands the service provider's perceptions of the client's situation and facilitates information about the success of specific interventions. In matching services to need, the ability of an approach to provide an appropriate view of the client's situation, direct professional activities, and give information about the anticipated extent of success of those activities, is invaluable.

This chapter examines the social systems approach as applied to work with older clients. The approach will be defined and concepts delineated. Two case examples will be presented. The first will be used to exemplify social systems concepts. The second case study will be presented for the purpose of analysis from a social systems framework and to provide knowledge for the service provider concerning application of that framework.

THE SOCIAL SYSTEMS APPROACH

The following case example concerns an older family that experiences difficulties following the father's illness. The case study will be used to exemplify the social systems concepts.

Case Example 2.1

Robert and Mary Allen are 75 and 76 years old, respectively. They have been married for 55 years. They report that their marriage has been positive for both of them. Mr. and Mrs. Allen have lived in their own home in the same community throughout their marriage. The community in which they live is a small one and they have a number of friends and relatives living nearby, including their three children.

Mr. and Mrs. Allen see their daughter, Martha, age 50, most often. Martha is their only daughter and does not work outside of the home. As a result, she frequently drops in on her parents or speaks with them on the telephone. Martha is married to Jim Martin and they have three children, two of whom are teenagers. When the Allen family gathers for holidays and special occasions, it is usually Martha who helps her mother prepare. Martha occasionally runs errands for her parents and helps with heavy housekeeping tasks. Martha has enjoyed this role. Her involvement with her parents often takes place at her initiative.

The Allen's two sons, Rob and John, are both involved with their parents, but to a lesser degree than is Martha. Rob, who is 45 years old and single, takes Mr. and Mrs. Allen to a restaurant once a week, mows their lawn in the summer and shovels snow in the winter. John is 52 years old, married, and has two adolescent sons. He and his wife have Mr. and Mrs. Allen over for dinner once every other week. One of John's sons frequently stops by his grandparents' home after school to talk with them.

In addition to relatives, Mr. and Mrs. Allen have numerous friends in the community. They maintain an active relationship with their neighbors. If their neighbors suspect that they are experiencing a problem in any area, they will call Martha to alert her. Mr. and Mrs. Allen have attended the same church all of their lives. They continue to attend two church meetings weekly. Although quite a few of their peers are no longer living, they see the children of their deceased friends at church.

Three weeks ago, Mr. Allen fell and broke his hip and has been hospitalized since. He dislikes being in the hospital and becomes quite agitated when he talks about being hospitalized. He wants to return home and is concerned that he will be unable to do so. His physician has not discussed his condition with him, nor has he outlined what Mr. Allen can expect in the future. The nursing staff at the hospital is quite busy and, because of Mr. Allen's negative attitude about the hospital, spends as little time with him as possible. Mr. Allen, through his negative attitude, has discouraged the visits of church members and neighbors. Mrs. Allen is upset because of her husband's emotional condition. In addition, she is nervous about living alone and is also worried that her husband will be unable to return home.

Mrs. Allen has begun to worry about how she will take care of herself each day. She dislikes having to ask her children to do things for her, but is unable to drive because of poor vision. As a result, she relies on Martha to a greater extent. Martha provides transportation for Mrs. Allen to visit her husband in the hospital daily. Frequently, Mrs. Allen calls Martha to ask that Martha come to stay overnight, go to the grocery store for her, and carry out other tasks that Mr. Allen had previously performed. Martha's own family has begun to complain about the amount of time she spends away from them. She feels pulled between the needs of her parents and those of her husband and children. In addition, Martha regrets that she has less time for friends of her own and the church activities she had been involved in before her father's illness. Her brothers and sister-in-law can be available to help some evenings, but not during the day because of work responsibilities.

Mrs. Allen appears to have less enthusiasm about her family and her home than she did before her husband's fall. She and Martha occasionally have disagreements relative to running her home. Mrs. Allen's relationship to other family members is now characterized by tension. Following her visits with her husband, Mrs. Allen seems depressed. She is quiet on the ride home from the hospital and cries often. Mr. Allen expresses his feeling that his hip will not heal and that "they'll put me away somewhere." His outbursts toward family members have increased. Martha and John both feel that their relationships with their spouses and children are suffering due to the time they spend with their parents and the tensions that they feel.

In providing services to the Allen family, it is helpful to view them as a social system. Utilizing a social systems approach provides the practitioner with tools for analyzing the Allen's situation. The practitioner can examine the interactions of various members of the family, their impact on the family as a whole, and make a determination as to what services should be provided to whom.

Case Example 2.1 provides an illustration to which social systems concepts can be applied. The Allens are a couple with a history of successful relationships, both within the family unit and with nonfamily members. Their spouse relationship is satisfactory and their relationships with their children and significant others are good. In addition, their children and friends are positive about the help they provide for them. However, following Mr. Allen's hospitalization, several things have changed. First, Mr. Allen has difficulty believing that his situation will ever return to normal. Mr. Allen's pessimism influences his wife negatively. In addition, Mrs. Allen has concerns about her ability to function on her own. She is worried that her basic needs will not be met. Mrs. Allen is uncomfortable asking her children to carry out tasks that had previously been handled by her husband. She also, accurately, senses the stress her children feel as they must choose between commitments to her, their own families, and their jobs. As time progresses, Mrs. Allen is less confident and becomes more dependent. She is less able to encourage her husband and is more dependent on her children. The situation spirals and the stresses each family member feels have an influence on the family as a whole.

A service provider working with the Allens would benefit from information about how to intervene so that the Allen family's needs could best be met. However, it would be difficult to know where to start. Should the provider first work with Mr. Allen and hope that services to him would improve his attitude and result in Mrs. Allen becoming more confident? Certainly Mr. Allen's attitude has an impact on his wife, but her feelings of concern are *not only* the result of her husband's attitude. It may seem that Mrs. Allen should be the focus of the provider's concern. It is true that services provided to her will free her children to some extent. However, services are unlikely to exist that will meet all of Mrs. Allen's current needs. Clearly, there are a number of individuals involved in the situation and the behaviors of each have an influence on the entire family.

How can the social systems approach be helpful here? The social systems approach focuses on the *interactions* between individuals and/or larger social entities (Becvar and Becvar, 1982). Interactions between social systems produce dynamics that have an impact on those systems as well as on all other connected systems. A basic premise of the social systems orientation is that change in one part of the system influences the total system (Anderson and Carter, 1984). Consequently, action A does not cause behavior B to occur. Rather, behavior B is the result of interactions and responses to those interactions that have occurred throughout the system. Chain reactions do *not* exist. As Anderson and Carter (1984: 5) state, "causation is multiple and multidirectional." Behavior of one system is not determined by another, "but rather by the interaction and mutual causation of all the systems and subsystems" (Anderson and Carter, 1984: 5).

Therefore, we recognize that Mr. Allen's pessimism was not solely the result of his hospitalization, but also came from the lack of information he received from his physician, his relationship with hospital staff members, his concerns about his future, Mrs. Allen's lessened support due to her worries about meeting her own needs, and the concerns that he saw reflected in his children, as well as other interacting factors.

In order to understand and utilize a social systems perspective, certain basic ideas and concepts must be outlined. Those discussed below include social system, primary system, boundaries, linkages, energy, system maintenance, and organization.

Social system. A social system is a whole, complete in itself and made up of component parts. At the same time it is part of a larger whole. Consequently, each system is composed of *subsystems* and is also part, with other systems, of a *suprasystem*. For example, Mr. and Mrs. Allen, as spouses, are a social system. Individually, Mr. and Mrs. Allen are both subsystems of their spouse system. While their spouse system is a complete system in itself, it is also part of the larger Allen family system. That larger, suprasystem includes several subsystems composed of (1) Martha's family of husband and children; (2) John's family of wife and children; and (3) Rob; as well as (4) Mr. and Mrs. Allen.

Primary systems. Because a service provider's initial concern would be primarily with Mr. and Mrs. Allen, this couple would compose the system that would dictate the perspective of the provider. Consequently, the spouse system of Mr. and Mrs. Allen would be viewed as the *primary system* when examining the family unit. The Allen couple's system would be seen as a subsystem of their extended family. In addition, they are a subsystem of the church that they attend, interacting with other families and individuals who are participants of that system. They may also be a part of other systems within the community, such as the senior citizens center. Consequently, the system chosen as primary directs our attention to the various other systems with which it interacts as well as to that system's component parts.

Boundaries. How can a social system be identified? The *boundaries* of a social system allow the observer to identify a system and classify that system as distinct from other systems. The idea of boundary suggests that each social system is separate from others, has idiosyncratic characteristics, and can be identified as a specific entity. Within the boundary of a social system are the component parts that interact to make that system what it is. The observer is facilitated in locating boundaries by the fact that the interactions between the components of that system are more intense than are the interactions between those components and other subsystems (Anderson and Carter, 1984). Berrien (1968: 21) has defined boundary as

> that region separating one system from another; it can be identified by some differentiation in the relationships existing between the components inside the boundary and those relationships which transcend the boundary. It can be seen that the criteria defining the components are the same as those defining the boundary.

In other words, the relationships between the components, or subsystems, of a system are different from the relationships of those components with other systems. The Allen family, for example, is bounded by their interactions with one another as a family and by their identification with one another as members of the Allen family. In addition, the interactions of the Allen family are unique to that family and help to differentiate that family from other families. Therefore, the interactions between Mr. and Mrs. Allen would be characterized by different attributes than would a relationship between Mrs. Allen and a casual friend.

Linkages. The existence of boundaries does not prevent interaction between systems. Social systems are not static. They are dynamic, constantly relating to other systems in an attempt to continue functioning. When one system interacts with another, a *linkage* is formed (Anderson and Carter, 1984). The extent to which the boundary of a system is *open* or *closed* determines the amount of interaction that will occur between that system and other systems. A system that permits a large amount of input from other systems is more open than one that does not (Becvar and Becvar, 1982). It is imperative that a system allow input from other systems. If it did not, it would become rigid, unable to function, and cease to exist as a system. By the same token, a system cannot exist if its boundaries are completely open, or it would lose its identity as a system. An open system and a closed system (if they could exist as such) would be at opposite poles of a continuum. Berrien (1968: 23) has referred to the boundary of a system as a "filter," indicating that the boundary helps to define the system but does not prevent input from or output to other systems. Because systems are not static, they will each vary as to the amount of input from other systems that will be permitted to cross their boundaries. A system may be more open in one situation and less so in another. Mr. Allen is a good example of this. In his own home, with reasonably good health and numerous emotional and instrumental supports, he interacted with others in an open manner that contributed to his functioning. In the hospital, feeling uncertain about his future and perceiving a lack of emotional support from others, his boundaries were less open to those around him.

Energy. Anderson and Carter (1984) describe the interactions that take place between social systems as exchanges of *energy.* Through interactions with other systems, a social system both secures and expends energy in order to meet its goals. Energy exchanges occur between systems and among the component parts of systems. Energy exchanges provide systems with the input necessary to continue functioning. Energy exchanges take the form of *information* and/or *resources* (Anderson and Carter, 1984). Systems gain energy through information received and the resources available from their component parts and from other, external systems.

Without the exchange of energy, a social system would become stagnant and unable to continue functioning. For example, were Mr. Allen to become totally isolated, he would not receive the medical resources necessary to his physical functioning nor the support from his family that is necessary to successful emotional functioning. The fact that his family is less able to provide this support to him has been one factor contributing to his depression.

System maintenance. Social systems seek to maintain themselves with as little change as possible. Consequently, when an individual or family is faced with a crisis, they attempt to deal with that crisis by returning their situation to normal as quickly as possible. In this attempt, they expend energy to reach the goal of a return to the status quo. Reaching the goal provides the system with more energy to respond to other situations. A system that is not reimbursed for its expenditure of energy will lose energy and its ability to function will become less stable. In the course of its internal and external interactions, a system is constantly responding and adapting in an attempt to maintain itself.

Because of situational constraints, a system will be prevented from returning to its previous state. When this occurs, the system will seek to stabilize itself by adapting to its environment to the extent necessary for survival. However, the social system will adapt to the least extent possible in order to maintain the status quo. As Berrien (1968: 63) has suggested, "adaptations are responses to disturbances that may upset 'normal' relations. Adaptive systems are those which maintain their essential variables within those limits necessary for survival within the environments in which they exist." The inability to compensate for the loss of normality interferes with the system's maintenance of identity. Because each social system is unique, the concept of normality is different for each. In other words, what is normal for one system will not be for another.

In order to gain energy successfully, both from component parts and from external systems, a system must use the energy it has in a functional, organized manner. The goal of a social system is to gain energy from its internal parts as well as its environment. This energy is used to maintain its identity so that the system can continue functioning. If its subsystems are functioning well and are sufficiently organized, they serve to generate energy for use by the system (Anderson and Carter, 1984). Then the system has energy to use in its interactions with other systems. If the subsystems are in conflict with one another, they drain the energy available to the system and prevent it from successful interaction with the environment (Anderson and Carter, 1984).

The Allen family serves as an excellent example of this. Mr. Allen's concerns about his well-being, Mrs. Allen's fears, and the demands on Martha have prevented the family from successfully seeking outside sources of help. In fact, they have lessened Martha's ability to draw on the resources of her friends. As the situation continues, the family loses more energy and is less able to draw on the resources of those outside of that system.

By the same token, if the system is having difficulty in relation to its environment, it has little energy to utilize for the functioning of its subsystems. In the case of the Allen's, the lack of positive response from their physician, decreased interactions with neighbors and friends, and the difficulty that Mrs. Allen is experiencing in relation to Martha make it difficult for Mr. and Mrs. Allen to provide support to one another. *Consequently, a social system works in four ways to maintain itself: (1) gaining energy from its environment; (2) gaining energy from its subsystems; (3) meeting its internal goals (maintaining the order of its subsystems); and (4) meeting its goals through interactions with the environment. A breakdown in any one of those areas influences all other areas and interferes with the system's ability to function successfully* (Anderson and Carter, 1984). As a result, social systems attempt to organize and maintain some control over their internal parts and to have some control over their interactions with other systems so that they can gain energy and utilize it toward fulfilling system purposes.

Organization. As noted, social systems require some degree of organization in order to utilize appropriately the energy they secure. Anderson and Carter (1984: 17) have stated that *"organization refers to the grouping and arranging of parts to form a whole, to a put a system into working order. System organization secures, expends and conserves energy to maintain the system and further* its purposes." Organization enables a system to put its energies to the purpose of gaining more energy. By the same token, the compounding of energy facilitates the system's ability to organize.

A service provider assigned to work with the Allen family could benefit from utilizing a social systems perspective. An awareness of the many factors that contribute to problematic, as well as positive, interactions would facilitate accurate assessment of the problem, as would an examination of the various systems involved, both internal and external to the family. A determination of how family members are securing and expending energy would provide information about the family's attempts to maintain itself through internal and external interactions. Information about the Allen family has been presented to illustrate social systems concepts. In the following section, those concepts will be applied to a second older family.

THE PROFESSIONAL'S USE
OF SOCIAL SYSTEMS

In this section we will examine the application of a social systems perspective to work with elderly clients. A different case example will be presented and analyzed from a social systems orientation. This will be followed by a discussion of how the service provider can utilize this approach in practice with the older clients described in the example.

Case Example 2.2

Mr. and Mrs. Ryan, ages 66 and 65 respectively, have been seeing a counselor at the community mental health center for six weeks. They initially contacted the center following a referral made by their physician. The physician had referred the couple because of Mr. Ryan's complaints about conflicts in the couple's relationship that appeared to be affecting his health.

At the time of the initial contact, Mr. and Mrs. Ryan had both come to the mental health agency. The presenting problem was that Mr. and Mrs. Ryan had been married for two years, both having been widowed prior to that.

Since the time of their marriage, they have had numerous conflicts over various issues. Following each disagreement, Mr. Ryan has become ill. When questioned about the content of their conflicts, Mrs. Ryan stated that they seem to argue about three areas: the manner in which money should be spent, Mr. Ryan's children, and Mr. Ryan's involvement with friends from his first marriage.

The disagreements over money were focused on Mrs. Ryan's concern that Mr. Ryan is not careful with their funds. Prior to their marriage, they each placed a certain amount of money in a trust and agreed to live on the remainder of the money each had as well as on the income each received through social security and pensions. Both partners contribute approximately an equal amount monthly. Mrs. Ryan stated that Mr. Ryan spends money without discussing it first with her. When this has occurred, she has become angry and they argue. Mr. Ryan felt that his wife was too involved in his day-to-day spending habits and resented this. Some of their arguments over money took place in the counselor's office. Mrs. Ryan began the arguments by accusing Mr. Ryan of overspending, doing things behind her back, and not considering her goals in relation to money. Mr. Ryan responded to his wife by talking in a loud voice and denying her accusations. Neither individual was direct in sharing feelings with the other and neither showed an awareness of what the other was feeling. During the arguments, Mrs. Ryan consistently took the offensive, with Mr. Ryan becoming angry but defensive. Following each argument, Mr. Ryan would state that his chest hurt and Mrs. Ryan would become quite concerned about him, telling him that she was sorry and did not mean anything she had said.

The couple's disagreements about Mr. Ryan's children seemed have similar characteristics. Mrs. Ryan would accuse Mr. Ryan and when he became ill, Mrs. Ryan would apologize. The content of Mrs. Ryan's accusations were that Mr. Ryan preferred his children's company to hers. She indicated her feeling that he is "too close" to his children. She stated that he spends too much time with them and too little time with her. She was also concerned that Mr. Ryan's children were "turning him against" her, although she could not describe how they were doing this.

Similarly, Mrs. Ryan resented the time that her husband spent with old friends. She felt that he should not want to see friends from his previous marriage and that in seeing them, he was being disloyal to her. Mr. Ryan would not discuss this with his wife, but continued to see these friends.

At the time of the first meeting, both parties stated that they wished they could get along better. Mrs. Ryan indicated that she felt the counselor should help them to do this by "keeping my husband in line. You know, helping him to do the sort of things a husband should do." The counselor explained that she could not "keep people in line," but that she would be willing to work with them relative to the conflicts that they were experiencing. The primary goal that the three agreed to work toward was to talk about the disagreements that the couple had in order to develop more functional ways of disagreeing. It was agreed that Mr. and Mrs. Ryan would both work toward expressing feelings in a way that would facilitate resolving conflicts rather than increasing them, and that both parties would look at the three areas where most of the conflict was focused and work toward some sort of resolution in these areas.

During the five following sessions, it became more and more obvious that Mrs. Ryan was concerned that her husband would reject her in favor of his children and his former friends. Mrs. Ryan had few friends and was very dependent on and possessive of her husband. Her possessiveness seemed to him to indicate a lack of trust and frustrated him. His response to this was to become more remote and unavailable to her. Mrs. Ryan would then feel that her worst fears were confirmed and she would become more possessive.

Analysis of Case Example 2.2. When examining the Ryans' situation, it is necessary to recognize that the problems that they are experiencing are *multidirectional in cause.* None of the problems— Mr. Ryan's use of money, relationships with others, or Mrs. Ryan's accusations—is the sole cause of the difficulties that the couple is experiencing.

In order to analyze the case, a *primary system* will be chosen. Which is the logical system to focus on when evaluating this case? The observer has several choices. The focus could be placed on Mrs. Ryan, since she is the individual who is verbalizing the most dissatisfaction with the relationship. Mr. Ryan could be chosen as the primary system as Mrs. Ryan has indicated that her problems would be solved if his behavior would change. Attention could be directed toward both Mr. and Mrs. Ryan, as the problems that are experienced appear to have an influence on them both. Mr. Ryan's children are also involved to some extent, and they, with Mr. and Mrs. Ryan, could be the social worker's focus of choice, as could Mr. Ryan's friends.

For this analysis, Mr. and Mrs. Ryan—as a spouse system—will be the primary system of focus. Viewing them as the primary system will determine our perspective for examining other, related systems. The spouse system has been chosen for primary focus for several reasons. First, centering attention on either spouse does not acknowledge the fact that both of their interactions are contributing to their difficulties. In addition, focusing on either Mr. or Mrs. Ryan would support the notion that one individual in the relationship is the cause of the problems that they are experiencing rather than attempting to enhance the interactions between the two.

Second, as subsystems of the spouse system, Mr. and Mrs. Ryan are facing a number of issues that influence both directly. The issues of money, of how Mr. Ryan spends his time, and of who controls the relationship all have an effect on both individuals. Third, the other individuals involved with Mr. and Mrs. Ryan would best be viewed as systems that interact with the Ryans. Although interactions with these systems are significant to the Ryan's functioning, it is Mr. and Mrs. Ryan who are most directly experiencing the problems of concern. Choosing the spouse system as the system of primary focus draws our attention to interactions of the subsystems, Mr. and Mrs. Ryan, as well as to all other systems with which they interact and of which they are a part.

The *linkages* between the subsystems (Mr. and Mrs. Ryan) and between the spouse system and other systems are important units of analysis. It is through these linkages that the Ryans secure and expend energy in an attempt to maintain themselves as a system. Mrs. Ryan appears to have few linkages with systems other than her linkage with her husband. Certainly on a day-to-day basis she encounters other individuals and interacts with them, but it would appear that her *boundaries* are not open to allow other systems much impact on her or to allow her to have much affect on these other systems. She does not have children of her own and her relationships with family members are not strongly established. Her primary relationship is with her husband. However, even in this relationship, her boundaries are fairly rigid. She lacks flexibility in response to inputs from her husband. On the other hand, Mr. Ryan appears to have meaningful relationships with a number of other individuals. He has, over the years, established linkages with friends and children. These relationships are important to him and con-tribute to his functioning as an individual. Mr. Ryan's boundaries appear to be more open to exchanges of energies with systems external to the spouse system than to energy exchanges with his wife.

As with any system, the spouse system we are examining maintains itself through gaining *energy* from its subsystems and from its environment as well as through using its energy to meet its goals internally and externally. As noted above, a breakdown in one of those tasks will negatively influence the system's performance in the other task areas. The fact that the Ryans are currently having difficulty in relating to one another would direct us to look at the status of each of these task areas.

The couple does not relate to other systems as a spouse system. In fact, their relationship with the counselor is one of the few interactions the couple has had jointly with other systems. Mr. Ryan, as noted, does interact with several other systems: his children, friends, neighbors, and church acquaintances. These interactions with systems external to the spouse system are successful in that they make energy (in the form of emotional support) available to Mr. Ryan. Through his relationships with others, Mr. Ryan gains energy to meet his goals as an individual. He has been able to make necessary adaptations to maintain the relationships that he has developed. Because he is meeting his goals externally and thus gaining energy externally, Mr. Ryan has energy to contribute to his relationship with his wife. Mrs. Ryan, however, gains little energy through interactions with others outside of the spouse system and consequently has little to invest in her interactions with her husband.

The usable energy that the couple has must be spent to deal with the conflict between Mr. and Mrs. Ryan. It would appear that the energy gained externally by Mr. Ryan is being used at a rate faster than he can secure it. The energy gained externally is being spent on disagreements within the spouse relationship. The Ryans' internal goal would be to maintain themselves as a couple. For this to occur, internal conflicts must be minimized so that energy can be gained to meet the system's external goals. Therefore, their disagreements require some resolution so that they can be freed to work together to build internal resources. However, this is hindered in part by Mrs. Ryan's attempts to maintain her own personality system in a rigid manner and by Mr. Ryan's lack of productive communication with his wife. The energy spent on internal conflicts prevent them from making appropriate adaptations to one another or, as a spouse system, to their environment.

The energy that is brought into the spouse system requires more *organization* than is provided. Some organization exists, or the couple would not be able to maintain themselves as a system. The spouse system in this case is not sufficiently organized to conserve energy and further its purposes. It is because of insufficient organization that the Ryans are not utilizing more efficiently the energy that they have.

One aspect influencing the disorganization in this case is the struggle for control in the relationship. Mrs. Ryan attempts to gain control through the accusations made to her husband. Mr. Ryan appears to seek control through his physical complaints *and* through not discussing his wife's concerns with her. The lack of direct, honest communication is another factor preventing both individuals from gaining sufficient energy from the other. The energy that is gained is invested in continued conflict.

Application of the social systems approach. The counselor providing services to Mr. and Mrs. Ryan has begun the relationship by gaining information about the presenting problem, their inter-actions with one another and with other relevant social systems. Through gathering information, she has discovered that Mr. Ryan has a close relationship with his two children. The children used to stop by his home, but since his marriage they have indicated that they feel unwelcome there. Mrs. Ryan stated that she resented their visits and did try to discourage them from coming so often (once a week). Currently, Mr. Ryan goes to one of his children's homes for dinner once a week. Mrs. Ryan is always invited, but refuses to join him.

In questioning the Ryans about friends, the worker discovered that Mr. Ryan goes out for coffee with friends two mornings a week. Again, Mrs. Ryan is always invited to join, but refuses to do so. Mrs. Ryan stated that she has no friends of her own, but on closer questioning, it was discovered that she belongs to a women's group that meets weekly. She attends infrequently. In addition, a neighbor calls to talk with her on occasion.

The analysis of the Ryans' situation has provided the counselor with information about linkages between the Ryans and other systems, about the extent to which their boundaries are open, about their use and expenditure of energy and the extent to which the spouse system is organized.

The two goals that were established with Mr. and Mrs. Ryan were (1) to develop more functional methods for disagreeing by ex-pressing feelings in a manner that reduces rather than increases conflict, and (2) to work toward resolution in the three areas where conflict is currently focused. The Ryans and the counselor have agreed to work toward one goal at a time and choose the first goal for their immediate focus.

It is the counselor's perception that to accomplish this goal, the spouse system requires additional external energy that can be applied to the reduction of internal conflict. The external energy (resources and information) that is currently available is not being used to enhance communication between the two parties but rather is being spent randomly on conflict between Mr. and Mrs. Ryan.

The counselor began by developing a relationship of trust with both Mr. and Mrs. Ryan. Her purpose was to interact with them in a manner that would contribute external energy (in the form of emotional support, positive communication, and facilitation in decreasing internal conflict) to their spouse system. Because Mrs. Ryan had requested help from the counselor and had begun the relationship by viewing her as a potential ally, she was open to energy inputs from the counselor. The counselor supported her by listening to her concerns, showing respect for her, and encouraging her participation. Mrs. Ryan responded to this by verbalizing her fears about her husband's rejection. As Mr. Ryan was present, he heard his wife express her fears. He indicated his wish to include her in his life and noted that his invitations join him with children and friends had been sincere.

Throughout the counseling process, the counselor was a source of external energy to the couple. Mrs. Ryan slowly responded to the support she received and was able to continue to express her fears. However, particularly during the beginning sessions, she did not listen to her husband's concerns nor would she accept his statements that he cared for her. Later, however, she did agree, at the counselor's suggestion, to begin attending her church group on a regular basis and to return her neighbor's friendship. As she engaged in activities with and received some support from others, her demands on her husband lessened. She slowly allowed herself to hear his feelings and to acknowledge their legitimacy. When the counselor pointed out that each was listening to and responding to the concerns of the other on a more appropriate level, it was decided to move to the second goal of working toward resolution of the three major conflict areas.

Because Mrs. Ryan had become open to interactions with three additional systems—the counselor, her neighbor, and her women's group—and because these systems provided support to her, she was more open to her husband's concerns and needs and felt less threatened by them. Her decreased demands on Mr. Ryan and her increased willingness to let him hear her fears facilitated his willingness to make some adaptations for her. In addition, he requested his children to share with her their desire to be involved in her life. When they agreed, this served as another source of support for Mrs. Ryan.

As external energy was increased and appropriately utilized by the Ryans, they had more energy to deal with internal conflicts. With the counselor's support, they were able to become a more organized system and to secure energy from within the system as well as externally. As energy became available, internal and external goals were met and more energy was generated.

CONCLUSION

Within this chapter, social systems concepts have been presented and applied to case examples. The social systems approach is valuable for work with older clients and/or their families. This approach provides the professional with a framework for viewing the interactions between clients and their social networks. It allows the human service worker to gain information concerning the most appropriate resources and methods to utilize when meeting clients' needs. Application of the social systems approach directs the practitioner to examine the many and varied factors that exacerbate or alleviate the needs of older clients. This sets the stage for clients to be understood as unique individuals with numerous aspects that contribute to their functioning. Chapter 3 will focus on knowledge about the internal and external systems of the elderly.

3

INTERNAL AND EXTERNAL SYSTEMS
OF THE ELDERLY

The elderly individual can be viewed as a social system with internal systems and linkages to external systems. The internal components of the elderly include psychological and physical aspects. Social, financial, and other environmental factors are external components that relate to the internal components of the elderly. As the elderly seek to maintain themselves within society, they exchange energy with other systems. These energy exchanges influence and are influenced by the adjustment of the subsystems of the elderly individual.

In an attempt to cope and adjust to the environment, certain needs must be met. If the needs of the elderly are not met, their ability to gain energy and achieve goals will be thwarted and maintenance of balance will be negatively affected. It is important, then, that the needs of the elderly are matched with resources available in the environment. Within this chapter, the needs of the elderly will be examined and resources available to match those needs will be discussed. For service providers working with older clients, knowledge of needs and resources is important. In later chapters, the manner in which resources can be applied will be outlined and relationships between resource providers and clients explicated.

NEEDS AND RESOURCES OF THE AGED

Basic Needs

What are the basic needs of the elderly? All individuals have similarities in the needs they experience. Lowy (1983) discusses McClusky's (1973) categorization of needs and delineates the types of needs individuals experience. These include *(1) coping needs; (2) expressive needs; (3) contributory needs;* and *(4) the need to have influence on external factors that affect our lives.* These needs are experienced by the elderly as well as by other age groups. However, for each age group the need may be brought about by different situations and require different responses.

As the elderly experience differences in life-style and as some develop limitations in physical abilities, adaptations are required. The need to *cope* by adaptation is necessary. The inability to adjust successfully to age-related changes prevents necessary securing of energy and attainment of goals. If coping needs are not met appropriately, other goals will be impeded. As Lowy (1983: 22) suggests, "unless these coping needs are met successfully, there is little power left with which to meet the additional human needs."

Expressive needs, for the elderly, refer to the need to engage in activities that provide pleasure. Achievement of a goal may not be as important as is the process of being involved in a task that enhances feelings of competence. Validation of competence facilitates the functioning of the older individual's internal components. Feelings of competence can derive from a multitude of activities, including relationships, and need not be exclusively work-related.

The meeting of *contributory needs* involves giving to others. As stated in Chapter 1, a value basic for service provision is the belief that the elderly have the responsibility of contributing to others. Not only is this a responsibility, it is also a need. The feelings that older individuals receive from giving to others, and to themselves, enhance their feelings of self-worth. Research indicates that reciprocity exists between the elderly and other individuals (Seelbach and Sauer, 1977). In addition to benefiting the self-concept, the ability to initiate and return favors to other individuals provides the older person with some power in, and control of, relationships. Without the ability to reciprocate in relationships, an individual has less control over relationships with others. If this is the case, energy is more difficult to gain and goals are less achievable.

As a result, the fourth need, *exertion of influence,* is important. Lowy (1983: 23) states that without the ability to influence others, "we would be unable to meet our basic coping needs. . . . Older people want to continue to enjoy a sense of mastery and autonomy and exert some measure of control over certain aspects of their life-space, even those who are residents of total institutions." The need to be self-determining exists with older clients, as it does with any age group.

As we examine the specific needs of the elderly in relation to the more general ones described above, we will investigate the resources that can be matched to these needs.

Physical Status: Needs and Resources

For each of us, our physical well-being influences our ability to function. This is true for the elderly as well. The physical state of the elderly is of particular importance because of the physical changes that occur as people age. For the elderly, these changes increase their vulnerability to various illnesses (Okun, 1984).

Research concerning the physical status of the aged has indicated that the elderly experience a decline in health as they age. As the life span increases, more individuals live beyond 65 years of age. Today, there are eight times as many elderly individuals in the United States as there were in 1900, and 40% of those over age 65 are 75 years of age or older (Mayer, 1983). As individuals live longer, physical changes occur. For the elderly, physical changes may or may not be debilitating and do not necessarily result in excessive dependence upon others (Atchley, 1985: 67). We all depend on others to some degree. The idea that any of us, including the elderly, can live without some amount of interdependence is inaccurate (Springer and Brubaker, 1984; O'Brien and Wagner, 1980). However, it is the extent of that dependence that is at issue. The fact is that the majority of elderly live and function without excessive dependence on others, as do the rest of society, until the time of their deaths.

What are the physical changes associated with aging? As noted, disabilities causing dependency on others do not occur for the majority of the elderly. However, changes in physical functioning do occur for most older people. For example, eyesight often becomes less accurate with aging, as the older eye is less able to adjust to both light and dark and to make the transistion between focusing at close and far ranges (Okun, 1984). Other senses that may become less functional with age are hearing and tasting. The quality of sleep may decline as sleep patterns change. As a result, the older person may experience a reduction in both the duration and depth of sleep (Burnside, 1984). The skin of the older person becomes thinner and wrinkled (Burnside, 1984). In addition, muscle strength diminishes with age. Bones become weaker, from a loss in calcium. Blood pressure often rises as individuals grow older. Blood flow frequently is restricted due to atherosclerosis, which occurs when fat is deposited on artery walls (Weeks, 1984). Also, arteriosclerosis may occur, where the walls of the arteries become thicker and less resilient (Okun, 1984).

Due to physical changes, chronic diseases that the elderly are most likely to experience (and to experience at a much higher rate than other age groups) include arthritis, cerebrovascular disease, hypertensive disease, chronic sinusitis, arteriosclerosis, varicose veins, diabetes, frequent constipation, and hernia of the abdominal cavity (Jack and Ries, 1981).

For most older people, these diminishing abilities do not require extensive dependency on others and do not, to a great extent, limit their activities. Atchley (1985: 79-80) states,

Many heath care professionals, such as physicians and nurses, assume that a certain amount of limiting illness is normal for an aging person, an assumption that is *absolutely untrue*. Yes, limiting chronic conditions are common among older people, but many of these conditions are preventable, most are treatable, and all can be compensated for to some extent. Limiting physical illness is *atypical* of older people at any age.

If medical professionals expect all elderly to experience physical illness and extensive disabilities, attempts to prevent and treat these will be minimal. The percentage of elderly who experience pain and disabilities could be reduced if their physical problems were viewed as treatable rather than attributed to the natural progression of old age.

When compared to the rest of the population, the elderly experience a greater proportion of long-term, or chronic, ailments. As noted, these chronic conditions do not necessarily prevent successful functioning. Interestingly, the elderly experience fewer acute conditions (short-term illnesses or disabilities) than other age groups. However, when the elderly experience acute conditions, they are likely to have a longer duration than with younger age groups (Weeks, 1984; Atchley, 1985).

> The average number of days per year of restricted activity due to acute conditions is nearly three times greater for people aged 65 and older than for ages 17-44. So, though the average older person gets sick once a year, he or she is in bed 4.5 days during that illness and has his or her activity curtailed for 11 days. By contrast, a younger person is afflicted more than twice a year on average but spends less than 2 days in bed and restricts activity for only 4 days [Weeks, 1984: 229].

Weeks (1984) notes that acute illnesses may be more severe for the elderly because of the higher incidence of chronic difficulties, which can interfere with regaining health following an acute illness.

Although the majority of elderly can cope without the help of others, the service provider often comes into contact with those who cannot. For that small percentage of elderly who require extensive supportive involvement of others, the majority first seek help from family and friends. It is the individuals who do not have an informal support network or who require additional services beyond their informal network with whom the professional becomes involved. For older individuals whose health problems impede successful coping, the service provider can be a source of external energy and facilitate the functioning of the older person.

The physical state of the elderly individual may prevent him or her from satisfactorily meeting basic needs. For example, arthritis or poor eyesight could prevent an older person from engaging in a desired activity that could meet expressive needs. For an older person housebound due to physical difficulties, the need to contribute to others may seem difficult to fulfill. The feeling of lack of control over one's own body is likely to instill a belief that the older individual is powerless in other situations as well, including relationships with others. In order to meet these basic needs, the service provider benefits from an awareness of the resources available in society.

Resources for needs with physical origins. Numerous resources exist for the elderly whose needs stem from physical problems. As noted, informal resources are most preferred by the elderly when dependencies exist. Physical dependencies are no different. When physical and health conditions cause needs that the elderly individual cannot meet alone, they turn to family and friends. Each of the resources available to meet the physical needs of the elderly is provided through a social system. The systems providing resources have the potential to link with the older person and give energy that can strengthen the elderly person's functioning.

Family members and others in the older person's informal support network can and often will provide services for tasks that the aged may no longer be able to accomplish. For example, informal network members can complete household and yard tasks too heavy for the elderly, can provide transportation for an older person whose sight no longer allows them to drive, and can prepare meals for someone who can no longer safely operate a stove. In addition, family members and friends often open their homes to older relatives who cannot live alone. In 1975, 18% of persons over age 65 lived in intergenerational households (Brubaker and Brubaker, 1981).[1]

Some physical needs cannot be met by family members alone and family members are unequipped to meet some needs. For the elderly individual who requires regular medical services, the help of family members is inadequate. Some community health clinics have added geriatric services to existing medical services in an attempt to provide specialized treatment for older patients. Also, some agencies have initiated well-elderly clinics that provide examinations for the elderly and focus on preventive services. For those aged individuals who need services in their homes, nonprofit and proprietary visiting nurse, home health, and homemaker agencies function to meet needs (Gelfand, 1984). Visiting nurses, working in conjunction with a physician, can dispense prescribed medications, maintain health programs, and monitor elderly patients in their homes. Home health aides are able to provide personal hygiene services for the elderly, facilitate exercises, dispense medications prescribed by a physician, and monitor some physical conditions. Homemaker aides carry out household tasks and shop for groceries. Often the positions of home health aide and homemaker aide are combined in one person who completes both homemaker and health aide functions.

Elderly individuals who live alone and cannot cook for themselves can benefit from meals delivered to the home. Title III of the Older Americans Act provides for funding for meals delivered to the homebound. Home-delivered meals programs provide for one or two hot meals to be delivered daily to the home of individuals who are unable to leave home or to cook for themselves.

For those elderly who can leave home but are unable to maintain a balanced diet, nutritional meal sites provide physical as well as social sustenance. These programs, also provided for by the Older American's Act, are established for individuals over 60 years of age and their spouses. The focus of the programs is to provide nutritious food and socialization particularly for older persons with low incomes. The nutrition sites are often placed in areas where disadvantaged elderly reside. "Through this system, any variation of a means test is avoided, thus increasing the general acceptability of the program to the elderly, who often avoid programs that appear to be 'charity'" (Gelfand, 1984: 125).

Older persons who wish to remain in the community but cannot care for themselves during the day can benefit from adult day care programs. These programs are particularly helpful for those who have help in the evenings or perhaps live with younger families who are gone during the day. Adult day care functions to provide more than babysitting services for the elderly. Rather, it strives to enable the older person to maintain the greatest amount of independence possible (Gelfand, 1984). Adult day care programs may be administered by senior centers, nursing homes, hospitals, and mental health centers as well as other types of agencies. The agency in which the day care program is located is likely to determine its focus. For example, a day care program housed in a mental health center will likely stress mental health issues, while one located in a hospital attends to physical issues to a greater extent.

Another service that benefits elderly living in the community is the telephone reassurance line. In many communities, telephone networks have been established for the purpose of checking on the well-being of older persons. Some networks carry out their operations by having volunteers call elderly individuals to check on them each day. Others are set up as phone trees where one elderly person calls another who then calls the next person on the list. If a breakdown in the calling system occurs, individuals not called begin calling those scheduled to call them. Telephone reassurance programs may be voluntary, as noted, or may be carried out by paid staff, funded either by private or public agencies.

In addition to telephone reassurance lines, other programs have developed that provide assurance to elderly living alone in the community. For example, some hospitals have established monitoring programs. Through these programs, buttons are provided for the elderly to wear that, when activated, alert hospital emergency personnel to a crisis in the older person's home. An attempt is made to contact the elderly person at home. If the contact cannot be made, the hospital sends medical personnel to the home to investigate the problem. This type of program allows some frail older persons to continue to live at home with a sense of security.

Many health services for the elderly are funded by Medicaid and Medicare. Funding for Medicaid is provided through Title XIX of the Social Security Act. Medicaid programs are administered at the state level and consequently, services and eligibility vary from state to state. Medicaid provides for the costs of medical care for low income elderly as well as for other low income categories of individuals (Federico, 1983).

Medicare is administered at the federal level, authorized by Title XVIII of the Social Security Act, and provides for equal access to resources for all elderly in the United States. Medicare functions to provide hospital insurance to individuals over 65 years of age. In addition, those eligible for Medicare may choose to pay a small amount monthly in order to qualify for supplementary medical insurance. Supplementary medical insurance provides for partial (80%) payment for charges (deemed reasonable) by physicians for medical services (Gelfand, 1984).

Each of the formal programs described above may be provided in conjunction with informal support systems. Provision of needed health services to the elderly can allow *coping* needs to be met as individuals adjust while maintaining the most independence possible.

In addition, caring for physical needs may free the older individual to meet his or her *expressive needs* and maintain or regain a sense of *competence*. For example, an elderly woman may be unable to care for herself during the time her adult children are at work each day. An adult day care center may allow her to adjust to her physical situation and remain in the community. It may also provide her with activities that permit some expression of inner feelings. This could include poetry sessions, needlework, or another form of expression.

Enhancing the health of the elderly can also provide them with the ability to meet the needs of others. The healthier the older individual is, the more able he or she is to meet the need to *contribute* to the well-being of others. Finally, individuals who have their physical needs met are less apt to be viewed as frail and vulnerable and more likely to be allowed to have *influence* in their relationships with others. Individuals with unmet health needs may lack the energy to influence others and particularly, to influence decisions others make about them. Health provides older persons with the strength to advocate for themselves and to engage in reciprocal exchanges that will allow them some power in relationships.

Psychological Status: Needs and Resources

Psychological functioning is an internal factor that has an influence on both internal and external success in gaining energy and reaching goals. It is often believed that as individuals age, they begin to lose intellectual abilities. Numerous beliefs also exist concerning the emotional functioning of the elderly. Ageist jokes about the elderly often focus on "senility" or the emotional problems that they are believed to experience.

In terms of intellectual status, the elderly as a whole vary among themselves as do other categories of individuals. Research concerning the intelligence of the elderly, as measured by IQ tests, reveals that the elderly as a group score lower than do other age groups (Horn and Donaldson, 1976). However, it has been suggested that the tests do not control for variables that may intervene with the scores received by older persons on IQ tests (Baltes and Schaie, 1976; Botwinick, 1977). For example, physical and emotional variables can influence the intellectual ability of the older person (Okun, 1984). Atchley (1985: 81-82) states that, in terms of intelligence, "The more closely a function is tied to physical capacities, particularly physical coordination, the more likely it is to decline with age. The more heavily a function depends on experience, the more likely it will increase and the less likely it will decline with age."

Socioeconomic background also has an influence on intelligence scores. Beaver and Miller (1985: 15) report that "people who are raised in advantaged socioeconomic environments are more apt to attain high levels of intellectual functioning and to maintain such functioning into old age." Flexibility in both life-style and perceptions in middle-age has been related to better intellectual performance in old age (Beaver and Miller, 1985). Creativity, as well, has been linked to other factors such as self-identity, environment, and life-satisfaction (Okun, 1984). Consequently, intellectual functioning is influenced by (and influences) other systems.

Elderly persons who experience intellectual dysfunction are frequently thought to be suffering from organic brain syndrome. However, this is not necessarily the case. The majority of intellectual dysfunction experienced by the elderly can be alleviated. The belief that aging brings about damage to brain tissues is a prevalent one. *However,* symptoms of organic brain syndrome are exhibited by only 15% of the elderly population (Edinberg, 1985). Symptoms of organic brain syndrome include a disorientation to person, place and time, as well as a loss of memory, difficulties in decision making, and changes in an individual's emotional affect (Edinberg, 1985). It has been suggested that the majority of persons with organic brain syndrome are suffering from Alzheimer's disease (Weeks, 1984). Alzheimer's disease results from deterioration of brain tissues and causes losses of memory, deterioration of intellect, and personality changes.

Differences exist among researchers concerning *memory* and the elderly. Although the research indicates that some memory loss is associated with age, not all researchers agree that memory decline is age related (Schonfield, 1980). Other differences in opinion are related to the causes for memory decline. Memory involves recalling information learned. It is uncertain whether memory losses are the result of difficulties that occur prior to information input, during the process of receiving information or following acquisition of information (Schonfield, 1980). Although memory loss becomes obvious at the postacquisition stage, more research is needed to determine whether this is the stage in which the difficulty occurs.

In addition to the process of information acquisition, it is important to note when the information input occurred. Both short-term and long-term memory are believed to decline somewhat with age and short-term memory has been shown to be the least effective in the elderly. However, researchers also disagree concerning this. For example, recent research has found few differences between young and old in terms of short- and long-term memory concerning information *that was of importance to the respondents* (Botwinick and Stroandt, 1980). Weeks (1984: 71) suggests that the elderly may experience "differential motivation . . . to remember information that may seem trivial to them but less so to younger subjects." Also, health, intellectual, and emotional status may influence the ability to remember. In the same way, emotional status is related to physical and social functioning.

When studying the aged, it is necessary to recognize that personality factors have an influence on and are influenced by emotional status. The personalities of older persons are as varied as are those of other age groups. Theories concerning the adjustment of the elderly to later life have focused on how the older personality responds to the changes of old age. Research supports continuity theory that suggests that individuals, throughout their lifetimes, develop patterns of responses to various situations and that these patterns continue into and throughout old age.

Therefore, behavior in old age is viewed as a result of a person's life experiences and to the developed patterns of responses to those experiences. Individuals may meet with new situations in old age, but their responses are not unlike those to previous, similar situations (Neugarten, 1964). Adjustments will be made to each experience based on the pattern of response developed. With adjustments, some changes may also occur in developed response patterns, although patterns will likely remain recognizable and congruent with the personality of the older individual. The patterns of response that the older individual utilizes will interact with that person's environment. Consequently, appropriate responses to situations throughout the life cycle are "likely to have created a positive personal social environment and will thus facilitate the necessary current changes" (Wigdor, 1980) required by present life situations.

Other theories have focused on the *tasks* of individuals when they reach old age. Eriksen (1963), for example, viewed life as being composed of a series of developmental stages, where tasks accomplished at each stage influence functioning at the following stage. Eriksen envisioned the mature adult at the stage where conflict exists between integrity and despair. For those elderly who achieve integrity, their life, as they have lived it, is accepted as a meaningful part of their existence (Okun, 1984). For those who do not accomplish this successfully, despair occurs. Older adults who experience despair "fail to achieve ego integrity, they will look back on their lives as a series of missed opportunities and missed directions.... For such individuals, the inevitable result is a sense of despair about what might have been" (Beaver and Miller, 1985: 32).

The specific tasks that the older personality must face differ from those encountered during earlier years. The older individual may be forced to deal with physical, financial, employment, social, and housing changes. There are various potential responses to these differences as they occur in one's life. For example, as friends, spouse, or similarly aged friends and family members die, the older person's social support network narrows. The possible responses can include grief, guilt, anger, and/or withdrawal (Brubaker, 1985). Some elderly may feel guilt or anger at the circumstances of their lives. As the older individual reviews his or her life, guilt may result from perceived failures and relationships badly handled (Butler and Lewis, 1982). Integrity may be accomplished by those who are able to forgive themselves for the situations that they regret.

Review of past behavior and the experience of current losses may result in depression for the older person. The elderly experience depression more than do other age groups (Butler and Lewis, 1982). The symptoms of depression displayed by the elderly may be different than those of younger individuals. For example, the elderly are less apt to exhibit low self-esteem and more likely to display inappropriate pessimism when depressed than are other categories of individuals (Blazer, 1982). Blazer (1982) states that the elderly have a higher rate of suicide, although they make fewer suicide attempts, than any other age group. The attempts made are more serious and successful.[2]

The elderly also face the task of maintaining independence. At times, this may contribute to feelings of loneliness. As Herr and Weakland (1979) suggest, independence for the elderly may be achieved at the price of loneliness. The determination to be self-sufficient may preclude caring others from becoming involved (Butler and Lewis, 1982).

It must be remembered, however, that as a whole, the elderly function successfully emotionally. Their emotional responses to the similar situations they face are partially determined by the patterns of response that each older person has developed over his or her lifetime.

Resources for psychological needs. The resources that exist for the emotional intellectual subsystems of the elderly are varied. These external systems are a source of support that can enhance the goal achievement of the older person. For older individuals who experience difficulties in the areas of learning and memory, several aids exist. Although it is unknown at what stage of learning the elderly experience difficulties that preclude accurate remembering, it would be helpful for the elderly to strive toward "stronger habit formation, overlearning, and improved procedures at the time of registering information. There are no exceptions to the general rule for all organisms of all ages that better learning produces better remembering" (Schonfield, 1980: 220-221). Skinner (1983) has suggested that the intellectual functioning of the elderly can be enhanced through rehearsing what will be said in certain situations, using cues to remember, and making time for leisure that will reduce mental fatigue.

For those older individuals who experience intellectual and emotional problems, resources exist in the form of community mental health centers, aspects of senior center programs directed toward mental health, programs housed in long-term care facilities, and nontraditional types of programs (Sargent, 1980).

Unfortunately, the community mental health centers that provide services specifically geared for older clients are in the minority. Several reasons for this exist. First, more older individuals require mental health services than there are professionals trained to provide therapy to the elderly (Kay and Bergmann, 1980). Second, the psychological problems experienced by the elderly are often viewed as part of aging and not treatable (Gelfand, 1984). For example, Ginsburg and Goldstein (1974) found that physicians seldom refer older patients to psychotherapy because they feel the elderly would not gain from these services due to their age. Third, professionals often prefer not to work with older clients. Garfinkel (1975) surveyed psychotherapists from different professional backgrounds and found that the respondents generally believed that older individuals are not talkative. Garfinkel states, "Here we see what may be a new, insidious stereotype insulating the 'reluctant therapists.' . . . By denying the older patient's need to communicate, the therapist excludes him from any sort of meaningful relationship" (1975: 127).

The elderly themselves may avoid treatment because of stereotypes they hold about mental health services or because of lack of access to existing services. Community mental health centers that provide outreach programs for the elderly and employ knowledgeable, competent gerontological psychotherapists can provide energy to meet the needs of the elderly experiencing mental health problems.

As older individuals develop relationships with staff members in senior centers, they or their families may approach staff with mental health concerns. Some senior center directors have training in the area of counseling and are prepared to work with seniors and their families. Other centers have developed peer counseling programs to allow center participants to receive support and help from their cohorts.

Other resources for the elderly and their families include nontraditional types of therapy programs and self-help groups (Sargent, 1983). Reminiscence groups have been utilized to promote both socialization and positive self-evaluation within various settings (Ingersoll and Goodman, 1980). Many programs include groups for families of the elderly as well. For example, support groups for family members of an older individual with Alzheimer's and groups for family members who are caretakers of older persons have been developed (Springer and Brubaker, 1984).

Many long-term care facilities employ social workers to deal with psychological difficulties experienced by residents. In this setting, social workers often utilize a psychosocial perspective, working with both the elderly resident, family members, and staff to enhance psychological functioning.

Service providers who successfully utilize mental health resources can provide an external source of energy that facilitates the psychological functioning of older clients. Individuals who cannot function successfully intellectually or who experience depression are obviously robbed of the ability to make appropriate adjustments to life tasks. Consequently, the energy taken by psychological dysfunction prevents successfully meeting the need to *cope*. The ability to be *expressive* may also be negatively influenced. Those older persons who are labeled "senile" by significant others will unlikely be allowed to meet the need of making *contributions to others*. Finally, those who suffer from psychological problems not only lack the ability to *influence* their relationships with others but also may be prevented from maintaining *control* over their own lives. As a result, guardianship by others may be established and decision making by the older person denied.

Financial Status: Needs and Resources

The financial status of any individual is relevant to his or her functioning. Without the income to provide for the basic necessities of life, individuals cannot cope physically and, often, psychologically and socially. Other basic needs are also influenced by the financial status of the older person. As individuals become elderly, they may require greater financial income than in late middle-age. For example, health problems may entail medical costs, previously unneeded household help may now be required due to an inability to carry out household tasks, or transportation requirements may be different if one is no longer able to drive. Kamerman and Kahn (1976: 319) report that the elderly "spend proportionally more on food, shelter, and medical care than other age groups."

Consequently, financial needs may become greater at the same time that the older individual is adjusting to a decline in financial resources. Due to retirement, many older families are faced with a fixed income. If economic inflation occurs, the financial plans made in earlier years become extremely important. The extent to which the elderly are financially able to support themselves influences the balance they achieve between dependence and independence (Okun, 1984). In addition to maintaining independence, a sufficient income is necessary to continue one's life-style into old age (Eisler, 1984).

What is the financial situation of the aged? According to U.S. census data, in 1983 the median income of families headed by individuals 65 years of age and older was $16,862. In 1983, the poverty level was defined as $6,023 for elderly couple households and $4,775 for the aged living alone. Of the elderly 65 and older 14.1% were below the poverty level. Interestingly, the poverty rate for individuals under age 65 was greater: 15.4% in 1983 (Fowles, 1984).

Elderly members of minority groups and those residing in rural areas are financially at a disadvantage. Older women, blacks, Hispanics, and those living outside of metropolitan areas have a greater probability of being below the poverty line than do men, whites, and individuals residing in metropolitan areas. Discrimination throughout their lifetimes place elderly minorities in a financially undesirable position. The fact that minorities may have been discriminated against in employment and income will in retirement negatively influence their social security incomes, pensions, and assets (Kamerman and Kahn, 1976). Some groups find themselves in double or triple jeopardy. For example, elderly widowed black women living in rural areas are at a particular disadvantage financally (Scott and Kivett, 1980).

As with any age group, there are variations in income with the elderly. For example, although 4.4% of households headed by persons 65 years of age and older had incomes of $5,000 or less in 1983, 5.7% of older households had incomes over $50,000 that same year (Fowles, 1984). Consequently, life-styles of elderly persons are varied. For example, some elderly live in subsidized housing or in other housing situations that reflect extreme poverty while others live in affluence.

Financial resources. Older individuals receive income from various sources. For noninstitutionalized elderly, income sources in 1982 included social security, private earnings, income from assets, pensions (public and private), and monies from sources such as unemployment and supplemental security income (SSI). Social security payments provided for 37% of income to the elderly, earnings made up 24%, income from assets was 23%, pensions gave 13% and income from transfer payments such as SSI provided 2% (Fowles, 1984).

The emphasis of the Older Americans Act is to provide an adequate income for the aged and to encourage elderly to remain in the community. As a result, resources are available that enhance the life-style of community-based elderly without the prohibitive cost that those resources might otherwise entail. Resources provided through the Older Americans Act are not based on the preretirement income of the individual elderly recipient. This is not the case with social security income. The amount provided by social security payments is determined by income prior to retirement. Consequently, an elderly person who earned little throughout his or her lifetime will receive little social security income in retirement.

Several programs serve to elevate the living standards of those individuals who receive little income. These include programs that provide cash directly to older recipients, such as SSI, as well as programs that provide services and benefits either at no cost or at a less competitive cost than in the free marketplace.

The SSI program came into effect in 1974. This program provides cash to older recipients. The program was developed for elderly, blind, or disabled individuals who, because of little income and assets, are able to pass a means test to qualify. As a consequence of SSI, elderly individuals with few other resources can depend on a guaranteed income (Zastrow, 1982). SSI is administered at the federal level. As a result, payments to recipients are consistent regardless of state of residence.

One source of financial aid for low income elderly is public housing. In addition, some elderly may also qualify for federally administered programs that supplement the rent of some low income individuals. Elderly recipients of these programs' services receive in-kind (as opposed to cash) benefits that supplement their incomes.

Transportation programs also benefit the elderly. Funded under Title III of the Older Americans Act, various senior centers provide transportation for aged individuals. In addition to providing transportation to those who are financially unable to maintain a car, the elderly who are physically unable to drive can also enjoy these services.

Medicaid and Medicare, both discussed under the physical resources section of this chapter, provide services to the elderly and indirectly supplement their income. These programs are a valuable financial resource for the elderly.

For the elderly who require nutritious meals but are unable to pay for them, nutritional meal sites, meals on wheels, and food stamps exist. Meal sites and meals on wheels programs are also discussed under the physical resources section of this chapter. The food stamp program provides for low income elderly as well and is administered by the U.S. Department of Agriculture (DiNitto and Dye, 1983). Requirements to qualify for food stamps are set at the federal level and are consistent across states. SSI recipients automatically qualify for food stamps. Other elderly whose income is low enough to meet a means test qualify for food stamps.

Homemaker-home health care services are often provided for older persons through various programs. For example, some of these services are funded through Title III of the Older Americans Act and are provided at no cost to recipients. The input of financial resources for the elderly potentially enhances the ability of older individuals to meet financial needs. This can facilitate the elderly in meeting basic needs, such as control over their environments.

Social Supports: Needs and Resources

Gerontological and practice literatures have suggested that professionals often lack knowledge about the social networks of their elderly clients (Blenkner, 1965). Shanas (1979a) suggests that programs and services for the elderly are based on a lack of information about the informal support systems that exist for elderly clients. Blenkner (1965) and Kosberg and Harris (1978) state that professionals may believe that older families do not provide help to elderly members because these professionals come into contact with elderly who do lack social supports. In addition, the beliefs of professionals may be related to some practice literature, which Miller suggests "seems to reflect a preoccupation on the part of most social agencies with the elderly who do not have families or have become isolated through dissolution of their family" (1981: 421).

However, gerontological literature, and increasingly practice literature, points to the existence of informal social support systems for older individuals. Gerontological theory suggests that individuals, upon reaching old age, do not abruptly change relationships or become isolated from informal support systems. Rather, the literature reveals that the old are likely to continue relationship patterns established and carried out throughout their lifetimes. This would include family relationships. (See discussion of Neugarten's continuity theory under the "Psychological Status" section of this chapter.)

Hess and Waring (1978) state that the importance of children to an individual in old age is likely to be similar to their importance in earlier years. In terms of the family's view of their aging member, it has been suggested that within the family, all of one's segmented social roles are consolidated to form a total person. Each family member is viewed by other members in terms of this consolidation of roles (Shanas, 1979a). It might be assumed that a change in some roles—retirement, for example—would not significantly alter the family's view of and relationships with the older member. Consequently, the aging person continues a relationship with the family and with other support systems similar to relationships in earlier years.

Theory is supported by gerontological research, which indicates that older persons maintain relationships with their adult children throughout the life span (Hess and Waring, 1978; Cantor, 1975; Shanas, 1979b), that both elderly parents and adult family members expect the adult family to perform tasks that will contribute to the welfare of the elderly parents (Shanas, 1968; Simos, 1975; Seelbach and Sauer, 1977; Shanas, 1979b), and that helping relationships exist between older individuals and their families (Reece et al., 1983; Kaufman, 1980,; Brody et al., 1978; Shanas, 1979a).

Shanas (1968), in a cross-cultural study of help patterns in three countries, found that in Britain and the United States adult children in white collar families tend to live apart from their parents to a greater extent than do lower class children and their aged parents. Little class difference was noted in Denmark. However, Shanas (1968) reported that although the amount of help adult children give their aged parents is influenced by social class, in all three countries and at all social levels aged parents receive help from their adult children.

Cantor (1975) approached filial responsibility by investigating cross-cultural support patterns of New York's inner city elderly and reported that familial relationships are strong between elderly parents and their adult children. A positive relationship was discovered between the amount of help aged parents receive from their children and the vulnerability (operationally defined by age and income) of the parents. Further, the findings of the Cantor (1975) research indirectly support the Shanas (1968) study. Cantor found that lower socioeconomic status aged parents tend to live more often with their children, while Shanas concluded that the greater the vulnerability of the aged parents, the more help from adult children will be forthcoming.

It is important to note that the elderly provide help to, as well as receive it from, their children. The desire and need to *contribute* does not change in old age. Sanders et al. (1984) report that the elderly engage in reciprocal relationships with their children and that they receive satisfaction from this. In addition, past and present reciprocal relationships appear to enhance the quality of care provided to an older parent by an adult child (Horowitz and Shindelman, 1983). Consequently, it would appear that past or ongoing contributions by the elderly may facilitate meeting the need to have some *control* over relationships. However, helping relationships between older parents and adult children arise not only from obligation but also from feelings of affection (Cicirelli, 1983).

A study that examined help patterns of urban, lower class families attempted to ascertain associations between aged parents' morale and help received from children (Seelbach and Sauer, 1977). It was concluded that elderly parents have expectations about the responsibility their adult children will take for them. Numerous studies indicate that when elderly parents are in need, their adult children respond in an attempt to meet those needs (Blenkner, 1965). For example, Simos (1975) explored aged parent-child relationships among Jewish families and reported that when older parents' physical and psychological difficulties require intensive care, adult children become involved. In addition, Shanas (1979b) states that the older individual who is ill finds that both immediate and extended family members are supportive.

Although community services are often available for the elderly, families have been shown to continue to provide those same services to their relatives (Shanas, 1979a). "Adult children traditionally have been the elderly's primary support system, and they continue to provide such help today—partly, because the elderly may believe that 'no one does it better'" (Seelbach, 1984). Anderson (1984) reports that widows first turn to their adult children when they have concerns to discuss, but they seek aid from siblings when they need physical or financial help.

The services provided by family members include provision for physical, emotional, and social needs (Bild and Havighurst, 1976). In fact, the elderly individual's informal resources are generally utilized before formal resources are called on (O'Brien and Wagner, 1980). The older individual's preference for family as opposed to agency service provision is only one reason for this phenomenon (Riley and Foner, 1968). Family members expect to perform services to meet the needs of their older relatives (Shanas, 1979a; Seelbach and Sauer, 1977; Blenkner, 1965). When services from formal organizations are required, family members act as a liaison between their aged relative and the community organization (Shanas, 1979b), carrying out tasks such as referral and follow-up, which the elderly person is unable to perform. Community service provision follows and adds to informal service delivery.

The gerontological research literature reveals that for some elderly individuals, family members live in close physical proximity. For others, family live at some distance, although supportive patterns are maintained. A recent investigation of elderly persons residing in inner New York City discovered that older respondents have children living close to them. In addition, there was "evidence of a mutual assistance system between generations" (Cantor and Mayer, 1978: 49). An investigation of older people in Cleveland, Ohio, found that 90% of the sample received some type of service from family or friends and 87% of the respondents indicated that they had someone to help if they became ill or disabled (Lebowitz, 1978).

Although the majority of older persons and their families prefer to live in separate households (Hess and Markson, 1980; Streib and Hilker, 1980; Shanas, 1979a; Wake and Sporakowski, 1972), most elderly persons reside near their relatives, as noted. Of elderly people in the United States 80% have living children, and 75% of those children live within 30 minutes of their parents (Blazer, 1978). Stehouwer (1965) studied older families and found that of the elderly who had living children, 80% of the older sample had seen an adult child in the week prior to the interview. For elderly with families in close proximity, the majority of needed help is provided by family members (Gross-Andrew and Zimmer, 1978). In fact, 80% of the home health care required by older persons in the United States is provided by relatives (Brody et al., 1978). Older individuals in long-term care also maintain relationships with their families

(Brubaker and Brubaker, 1984; O'Brien and Wagner, 1980; Hook et al., 1982). The visits of family to the elderly in long-term care enhance the well-being of the older family member (Greene and Monahan, 1982).

For those older persons with no living children, their support system may be composed of other relatives or friends. "Sibling relationships are important to older persons. It is a family relationship that endures throughout life even though interaction may diminish with age. Although adult children provide more assistance to older parents, older siblings help one another and are supportive of each other" (T. Brubaker, 1985: 83). Also, nieces or nephews may take the place of children in providing social support to the elderly individual.

Other sources of support include friends, neighbors, and those individuals whom the older person defines as family. Sussman (1977) refers to these persons as "fictive kin." Fictive kin might include close neighbors or other friends. Friendships as well as family relationships continue into old age. Atchley (1985: 149) notes that "most older people have at least one confidant with whom they have a close, intimate relationship." Gallagher et al. (1981-1982) point to the value of a confidant in facilitating the adjustment of a bereaved older person. The confidant may be an adult child (Kohen, 1983), a friend, or a professional. Service providers will undoubtedly encounter the minority of elderly who lack informal resources or who, for various reasons, do not interact with family members or friends. While the majority of elderly do have interactions with informal resource systems, some do not. It is this group of elderly who turn first to formal resource systems for services.

The literature does not deny that aged individuals and their informal support systems can experience stressful relationships. For example, some adult children have difficulty accepting their parents' dependence on them (Lowy, 1985). The fact that parents are becoming older may be difficult for adult children who do not understand the aging process (Johnson, 1978). Often adult children have their own families and the pressure of care for the old and the young for whom they are responsible becomes an excessive burden (Brody, 1981; Miller, 1981; Springer and Brubaker, 1984). Families who experienced relationship problems in earlier years are likely to experience similar problems upon aging.

Other conflicts may arise from the inability to adjust to the changes that result from having an aging member (Steinman, 1979). Also, the adult child's fear of aging may influence the relationship (Robinson and Thurner, 1979). At times, changes in established relationships pose problems for older families (Kirschner, 1979). However, the literature reveals that in most cases, despite younger family members' conflicts with other responsibilities, resentment at their parents dependence on them, or lack of understanding of the aging process, family members do provide help and support to their aged relatives. In spite of problems that may exist, expectations that help should be given are held by both older relatives and younger members.

Social resources. Although informal social supports are available to most older individuals, the elderly person's needs may extend beyond the support available. In the majority of situations, the family member primarily responsible to provide care to the elderly person is a woman (Springer and Brubaker, 1984; Steinmetz and Amsden, 1983). As more women are employed outside of the home, the responsibilities and expectations for them increase (Springer and Brubaker, 1984; Brody, 1981) These women not only support their older relatives, but may also have responsibilities related to children, spouses, and employers. While they may wish to be primarily responsible for the social support of their older relative, other demands on their time and energy may preclude their acting out that desire (Stroller, 1983). Other informal support systems may be composed of friends who have other obligations or who may be too elderly themselves to provide the amount of support needed.

When informal support systems that wish to help the elderly find the tasks involved overwhelming, the sharing of responsibilities with professional service providers is an option. Streib (1972) introduced the concept of "shared functions," suggesting that formal societal organizations and families combine their efforts in providing services to the elderly. Streib notes the advantages of this approach: allowing the elderly to have the support of informal support systems without feeling totally dependent on them, and giving the informal support systems of the aged freedom from feeling totally responsible for them. Blenkner (1969) also suggests the use of kinship *and* societal responses to the needs of the elderly. Sussman (1977) calls for the older person's family to act as a liaison between him or her and informal resource systems.

Often community resources alone are not sufficient to prevent institutionalization of the elderly. By the same token, adult families often lack the varied resources required to maintain elderly relatives in the community. The combination of resources available to both family members and professionals may provide the answer for the elderly at risk who wish to remain in the community. In fact, for housebound elderly, the combination of formal and informal services helps prevent institutionalization (Robinson, 1983).

McKinlay (1973) found that individuals who did not receive formal social services to the fullest extent possible used informal help from individuals within their social networks. McKinlay suggests that this is negative, indicating that these individuals are controlled by their informal support systems. However, individuals who rely heavily on formal social services could be viewed as being controlled by that aspect of their social network.

Older individuals may perceive themselves as most in control of their lives when informal and formal help is blended. When this is accomplished, a basic need is met. In addition, when older clients are allowed to participate by helping themselves whenever possible, and reciprocating in some way for services, *contributory needs* may be met. Bradshaw et al. (1980) state that both elderly clients and their families prefer shared support. Shared support may alleviate some of the pressure felt by family members (Zarit et al., 1980) while allowing family to give to the older member. It has been suggested that the addition of formal supports to family help can facilitate adult children in forming an independent-adult rather than a dependent-child orientation toward their parents (Hess and Markson, 1980).

Formal support systems available to the elderly include senior centers, where older persons can become involved in recreational and educational activities (Gelfand, 1984). Within the senior center setting, participants can engage in structured activities that allow them to develop new friendships and maintain old ones. Adult day care provides a setting in which the older person sees peers on a regular, daily basis. Nutritional meal sites also provide the opportunity for the development of supportive social systems through interaction with other older participants.

Other formal systems provide social support although this may not be their primary function. For example, a visiting nurse or a homemaker aide may be viewed by their older client as a source of social support because of the positive interactions that they have on a regular basis.

For those older individuals who are institutionalized, the social service worker provides emotional and social support to the older resident. In addition, other programs such as activity therapy exist to involve the resident with peers. As with community elderly, nurses and other facility personnel whose main purpose is to provide physical care often give social support to the resident as well.

In the community or the institution, the elderly can also become involved as resource systems to one another (Lawson and Hughes, 1980). For example, Retired Senior Volunteer Programs (RSVP) encourage the elderly to contribute help to individuals in need. Various senior centers have developed peer counseling programs that provide a source of formal support from another elderly individual. This help can extend to other older persons. Some long-term care institutions establish programs that structure situations encouraging the elderly to provide emotional and social support to one another through activities and group discussions.

Without the input of formal and/or informal social resource systems, the older individual lacks the energy required to meet basic needs. As the social world of the older person narrows due to the loss of significant others, other social resources must come into play to fill the gaps. The existence of social systems that provide resources are necessary to the older person attempting to *cope* with current situations.

SUMMARY

Within this chapter, the internal and external systems of the elderly have been explored. Four basic needs of older individuals were identified: (1) coping needs; (2) expressive needs; (3) contributory needs; and (4) the need to maintain and exert some influence over relationships. These needs were examined in relation to the physical, psychological, and social needs and resources of the elderly.

NOTES

1. We cannot assume that this percentage of elderly require physical care from family members. Some may live with family due to other needs. Others live with their families to provide help to children and grandchildren. For example, adult children may request an older parent to live in their home in order to provide babysitting help. As dual-earner families increase, it is not unrealistic to expect that older parents will live with their adult children for the children's benefit.

2. It is important to note that older individuals may be thought to be experiencing depression when this is not the case. For example, an older individual may show signs of depression such as boredom or irritability when the cause is not depression but rather, sensory deprivation (Wigdor, 1980).

4

INITIATING RELATIONSHIPS

The professional relationship begins with the first client contact, whether that contact takes place over a telephone or face to face. The manner in which the service provider approaches the client, or responds to the client's approach, will influence the quality and success of the relationship (Brubaker, 1983). This chapter focuses on establishing initial relationships with older clients and on the importance of the initial contact in regard to the overall professional relationship. The service delivery framework and the social systems approach, as discussed in earlier chapters, will be applied to the initial stage of the professional relationship with older clients. This chapter begins with information about *establishing professional relationships with older clients* and integrates this material with the *values, purpose, knowledge* and *tasks* appropriate for work at this stage of the service provider-older client relationship.

ESTABLISHING PROFESSIONAL RELATIONSHIPS

Konopka (1983: 91) has stated, "A good relationship makes honest communication possible and its quality determines whether treatment is effective or not." Certainly honest communication and effectiveness are important in professional relationships. As noted, a positive beginning between two or more individuals can facilitate the success of the total relationship. The quality of the relationship determines the boundaries established between service provider and client, which in turn influence the potential of the worker to provide input to the client system.

Various aspects are involved in beginning a positive relationship with elderly clients. The service provider facilitates development of a relationship by carrying out *values* through establishing a *purpose* for the contact, applying *knowledge* appropriately and utilizing skills in the *tasks* carried out. The following case example calls attention to several important factors.

Case Example 4.1

Mrs. Lipman's physician referred her to a local social service agency following her annual physical examination. Mrs. Lipman had told her physican that she lived alone and was having some difficulty in cooking her meals and in meeting some of her other household needs. In addition, the physican thought that Mrs. Lipman seemed disoriented at times during the examination. Mrs. Lipman agreed to call the social worker to whom she had been referred, but was unsure as to why her physician wanted her to call.

She did call the agency, however, and spoke with Mrs. Smith, a social worker. Mrs. Smith asked Mrs. Lipman why her physician had referred her. When Mrs. Lipman responded that she did not know, Mrs. Smith outlined the services her agency could provide and suggested that Mrs. Lipman might want to consider whether those services were appropriate for her needs. Mrs. Lipman said that she would do that and call back if she wanted to use the agency's services.

Mrs. Lipman did not call back. When the social worker followed up on Mrs. Lipman's call the following week, she found that Mrs. Lipman was not talkative and did not provide much information. Mrs. Lipman stated that she preferred to have her neighbors help her, although she did not know if they would be able to do so.

The initial contact between Mrs. Lipman and Mrs. Smith influenced Mrs. Lipman's feelings about a relationship with the social worker. Mrs. Lipman was unsure as to why she was to call Mrs. Smith and Mrs. Smith exacerbated that confusion when she did not talk with Mrs. Lipman about her specific needs and situation. Although Mrs. Smith may value enhancing clients' access to services and showing respect for clients, her response to Mrs. Lipman did not accomplish those ends. As a result, Mrs. Smith was unable to match resources to her potential client's needs.

Mrs. Lipman might have benefited from the services that Mrs. Smith's agency had to offer if Mrs. Smith had been aware of Mrs. Lipman's uncertainty in approaching her agency. Mrs. Smith's preparation for this initial contact would have included developing an awareness of some older clients' concerns when approaching social service agencies and a sensitivity to what clients are needing and wanting from the initial interview, both of which require knowledge about older clients and the ability to carry out this knowledge through task activity. Had Mrs. Smith been prepared in this way, she may have been able to gain the necessary information from Mrs. Lipman or at least to have obtained Mrs. Lipman's permission to contact other sources for needed information. A social systems orientation would have facilitated the social worker in asking the client about others who could provide information and who may be involved in contributing to or meeting the client's needs.

Mrs. Smith's outline of available agency services would have been appropriate had Mrs. Lipman requested that information, but she had not. Mrs. Smith could have requested Mrs. Lipman's permission to contact her physician in order to gain information about the reason for his referral, but this did not occur. In short, Mrs. Smith's response to Mrs. Lipman determined the texture of their future relationship as well as Mrs. Lipman's willingness and ability to receive services from Mrs. Smith and her agency.

Mrs. Smith's attempts to relate to Mrs. Lipman would have been facilitated had she responded to the client in the following way: "Mrs. Lipman, I am not sure how I can help you at this point. I would like to have more information about why your doctor told you to call me. Would you be willing to let me call and to ask his reasons for referring you to me?" Mrs. Smith could also gain more information about her client by asking if she lives alone or with others and by inquiring about her relationships with family and friends. Prior to this, Mrs. Smith should seek to reassure her client and allay any fears she might have about approaching a social worker. This could be accomplished by explaining that physicians refer people to her and that those individuals often have questions about her agency. Mrs. Smith might want to ask Mrs. Lipman if she has any questions that she could answer for her.

Service providers are most effective in initial interviews when they are prepared for first contacts with clients by having developed the following: (1) a *value system* appropriate to first contacts with older clients; (2) a *purpose* for initial contacts; (3) a *knowledge base* relative to the initial phase; and (4) specific skills to be applied to the *tasks* that carry out the values, purpose, and knowledge utilizing a social systems perspective.

VALUES

Regardless of client population, professionals must hold values that promote their clients' access to society's resources, uphold the dignity of their clients, and foster their clients' contributions to others in society. Several specific values flow from these general values when initially engaging in a relationship with older clients. These values include a belief that (1) clients have the right to place their *trust* in the human service worker; (2) the worker has the obligation to maintain *objectivity*; and (3) clients have the responsibility to *participate* in the helping process.

Trust. Trust is a necessary ingredient in the relationship between service provider and older client. It is trust that persuades individuals to reveal themselves to one another. Without the existence of trust, the older person will have little reason to seek the services of the service provider and the service provider will lack information concerning the client. Consequently, trust allows clients to use the professional as a source of energy and provides the professional with the potential to gain information about the ways in which the client utilizes energy and maintains balance.

What are the factors that *prevent* older clients from trusting a professional? First, older clients may have developed negative opinions concerning the helping professions. Second, a service provider's negative or faulty beliefs about the elderly may be conveyed to the older client. Finally, the client may have expectations of the service provider that are not fulfilled during the service delivery process.

Negative opinions about helping professionals may stem from a lack of knowledge about service provision. Often, older people have not needed formal resources prior to becoming elderly (Brubaker, 1983). For those individuals, trust may have to be earned by the professional. The older client who has not received social services previously may have already formed opinions as to what type of people helping professionals are, and these opinions may or may not be positive. It could be that the elderly individual has heard that service providers are difficult to deal with or that they impinge on the personal freedom of clients. Changing negative opinions to positive ones requires an adjustment on the part of the client. The service provider can become a source of external energy that allows the client to change. Negative opinions will be reversed only when service providers show, through actions, that they wish to enhance the client's ability to cope and to meet other needs.

Elderly clients are denied the right to trusting a service provider *if the provider has faulty beliefs about the older person*. For example, this may occur if the provider mistakenly believes that older persons are too frail, too elderly, or too disoriented to make decisions about themselves, particularly if that belief is conveyed to clients. Providers' beliefs may cause them to contact family members and other professionals without the permission of the older client or to make decisions about the older client without the client's input. Trust is enhanced when service providers' beliefs about clients allow the service providers to convey acceptance of clients and their capabilities and to establish confidentiality. Allowing older clients to meet their needs of expressing their desires, contributing to their own welfare, and gaining some control over the service provider-client relationship is basic to the establishment of trust. Some aged clients may not have these needs met through any relationship other than the professional one.

Unrealistic expectations on the part of the client can damage trust. For example, older clients without previous experience may believe that the service provider can solve all of their problems. In these situations, it is especially important for the practitioner to clearly outline what the limitations of helping are. In the same way, elderly clients who have had experiences with formal agencies in the past may also have difficulty or unrealistic expectations when establishing a trusting relationship with the service provider, depending on the character of those experiences, as the following case example illustrates.

Case Example 4.2

Mr. Gibson was a long-time community resident who had received general relief monies off and on since his early adulthood. In recent years he had received SSI and, as a result, had been visited on occasion by various caseworkers from the county welfare department. Although some of his experiences with the caseworkers had been positive, the majority were negative. After a visit from a caseworker, he usually felt that he should be able to be something that he was not. He also felt threatened in a vague way.

When a senior center was developed in his community, he knew little of its function. As part of an outreach program for the center, he was visited by the center's outreach worker and invited to attend. Because of his earlier experiences with formal helping agencies and their employees, Mr. Gibson was determined not to become involved in the center. The outreach worker visited Mr. Gibson on several occasions, treating him with respect. It was only after these visits and a clear explanation of the center's inability to place any restrictions on him personally that Mr. Gibson agreed to attend. He did not fully grant his trust at that time, but did tentatively allow a trusting relationship to begin with both the worker and the center.

In this case example, Mr. Gibson was expending energy by attempting to close his boundaries to any input from the outreach worker. If he had not gained trust in the worker, his energies would have lessened rather than increased. This would have interfered with achieving goals internally and externally.

By providing the client with a basis for trusting the worker, the client is allowed access to service, as clients are more willing to enter into a service relationship where trust is established. The outreach worker accomplished her purpose at the time of initial contact by conveying positive beliefs about Mr. Gibson and by clarifying the function of the center. In this way, Mr. Gibson began to change some of his negative opinions concerning social service agencies and his expectations became more realistic. Because the outreach worker began a trusting relationship at the time of initial contact, she will have a better opportunity to become a source of energy to Mr. Gibson as their relationship progresses.

The above discussion assumes that the client has the ability to participate in the service delivery process. There are of course frail elderly who lack that ability. When this is the case, the client should still be afforded the right to trust, through as much participation as possible. This can be accomplished by encouraging the most involvement of which the client is capable and also by clearly discussing with the client the steps that the service provider and others are taking when the client cannot be involved. Also, involving others whom the client can most fully trust and who can most fully represent their wishes (as suggested by Salzberger, 1979) will facilitate trust. This is exemplified in Case Example 4.3.

Case Example 4.3

Miss Kimler is a 68-year-old woman who has been diagnosed as having Alzheimer's disease. In addition to other symptoms, she is confused and disoriented to place and time. Miss Kimler has been referred by her sister to an adult day care program in her community. The director of the day care program received calls from Miss Kimler's physician and her neighbor following the sister's referral. The day care director determined that Miss Kimler has had a close, positive relationship with her sister throughout her lifetime.

The director of the day care program met with Miss Kimler following the referral. However, because of her extreme confusion, he also met with her sister at the same time. When Miss Kimler was unable to answer questions about her preferences for involvement in the program, the director asked her sister what she felt Miss Kimler would prefer.

Throughout the interview, Miss Kimler was treated with respect and made a part of the discussion. At the same time, an attempt was made to determine her wishes, as best known by her sister. Miss Kimler appeared to feel comfortable with her sister's responses and with the director's questions.

In the case example above, Miss Kimler's trust in the director (and potentially in the day care program) was facilitated by the involvement of her sister as a representative for her. By including her in the interview and also involving someone who Miss Kimler knew cared about her (her sister), the director not only ensured that Miss Kimler's desires were respected, but also that a trusting relationship was begun with Miss Kimler. It is important that steps are taken to gain the trust of those older clients who lack the ability to participate fully in the service delivery process.

When trust is established, linkages are formed between the service provider and client. As a result, the service provider can become a source of external energy for the client. For those clients whose energies were becoming depleted prior to the development of the relationship, the ability to accept and appropriately utilize resources may be limited. This external energy may allow clients to regain balance and to accept other resources the practitioner has to offer.

Objectivity. In addition to gaining the client's trust, it is important for the social worker to value objectivity when establishing a professional relationship with an elderly client, as with any other client. Pincus and Minahan (1973) state that objectivity is a basic component of the professional relationship. Objectivity involves professionals viewing both their clients and themselves realistically. In order to view clients objectively it is imperative that professionals are honest about their own feelings and needs. An awareness of themselves involves recognizing those issues with which they are uncomfortable as well as their need to control situations or avoid situations (Okun, 1982).

Brill (1985: 104) states that human service workers "must be aware of and deal with the distortion created by their own needs and desires, as well as their tendencies to see things as they would like them to be or to sit in judgment in terms of their own personal value system which may create a blindness all its own." Consequently, the professional, as a social system, must also adjust to the relationship with the client. Maintaining rigid perceptions about clients decreases the ability to interact with them.

It is possible for the service provider to become involved with personal issues related to aging and to project those concerns onto the older client or a client's family. Herr and Weakland (1979) note that counselors frequently make assumptions when working with older client systems. For example, a social service worker in a long-term care facility might be in the process of deciding whether to place his own mother in a similar facility because his mother is suffering from Alzheimer's disease. The worker might assume that the children of an incoming resident with Alzheimer's disease were experiencing feelings and concerns similar to his own. If he acted on that assumption, the new resident's children might feel misunderstood and avoid developing a relationship with him.

Other unresolved issues regarding parents or even grandparents can influence the service provider's initial relationship to clients if the provider is not aware of those issues. In the same way, professionals who have not dealt with their own feelings about death or dying may also have difficulty in developing a relationship with older clients (Brubaker, 1985a). Monk (1981) points to the difficulty that exists for social workers who have not resolved concerns about their own aging when engaged in a relationship with older clients.

Establishing the older client as participant. Various factors are involved in respecting the older client at the time of initial contact. Establishing the older client as a participant is particularly important. Whether or not the elderly client has been involved in a previous relationship with social service personnel, he or she may be unsure as to what role to take in the professional relationship. The messages given to older clients about their involvement at this stage of the relationship direct the clients' involvement at later stages. The participation of elderly clients in the service delivery process is as important as the participation of clients of any age. Denial of this opportunity can cause the client to lack investment in the relationship and any change that takes place will be accomplished at best without the client's approval and at worst against the client's will.

The aged client's participation in the helping process can contribute to the client's view of herself as a capable, effective individual. Lack of opportunity to participate can imply to clients that they are not capable of contributing to meeting their own needs. This has the potential to prevent clients meeting their contributory needs. Expecting participation implies a respect for the client and also may increase the client's access to resources. Moreover, clients who believe themselves to be capable of participating in meeting their own needs are more likely to view themselves as capable of contributing to others in society.

Clients are encouraged to participate when the professional clearly states, at the time of the initial interview, the expectation that the client is responsible for involvement in the service delivery process. Participation is maintained when the professional acts on this expectation, by providing alternatives and encouraging the client to voice opinions and make decisions about his or her life.

ESTABLISHING A PURPOSE FOR THE INITIAL PHASE

Initiating work with any older client requires that a mission or purpose be developed. The purpose should be focused on the specific needs of that individual. However, general priorities must first be developed that can be applied to various beginning contacts with elderly clients. These priorities can then be tailored to the specific needs of the individual client.

An emphasis on a purpose is particularly important when working with elderly clients, at this implies the belief that the client intends to and can change. The research literature reveals that some professionals approach older clients with the assumption that the client will not change due to his or her age or because change is not worth the effort, because the change "may be short-lived and that work with the elderly is an inefficient use of professional talents" (Kosberg and Harris, 1978). However, "one of the most powerful factors affecting the practitioner-client relationship is the expectation of change that the practitioner communicates to the client" (Keefe and Maypole, 1983: 29).

When the assumption that change cannot occur is operating, it is likely that the relationship will not be purposeful and may develop the characteristics of a friendship rather than of a professional helping relationship. If this happens, the client will not receive appropriate services delivered in an objective manner. Obviously a friendship involves meeting the needs of both participating parties in a reciprocal manner. A professional, purposeful relationship results in the service provider facilitating provision of the client's needs. The importance of purpose in a professional relationship has traditionally been stressed in the literature (Gambrill, 1983; Konopka, 1983; Pincus and Minahan, 1973).

The general purpose of an initial contact is to establish a relationship in which resources can be matched to client need. This involves interacting with the older client in a manner that enhances the client's ability to trust the worker and to utilize appropriately the services provided in subsequent stages. This goal requires the professional to form a relationship characterized by professionalism and to reflect service delivery values.

It is also important, at this stage, to communicate to the older client that there is a purpose for meeting together. Communication implies the belief that the client system is capable of adjusting to the current situation and that the service provider has a responsibility to make available resources that will enhance that adjustment. During the initial contact, a sense of purpose is established by asking clients their reasons for seeking the services of the professional, their perception of the problem(s) and what change(s) they would like to see occur. Methods for accomplishing the defined purpose require application of knowledge in completing tasks designed for this stage, as will be described below.

KNOWLEDGE REQUIRED FOR
INITIAL RELATIONSHIPS WITH
OLDER CLIENTS

Service providers engaging in a relationships with older clients require knowledge in several areas. First, *knowledge about elderly persons in general* is needed. Information concerning older individuals and particularly older clients is necessary in order to facilitate the initial contact with an older client. Second, service providers will benefit from gaining *information about the specific clients* with whom they will be meeting. This information allows practitioners to prepare accurately for older clients' concerns and questions that may arise at this point. Third, preliminary information about the *systems*, both formal and informal, with which clients are involved is valuable to professionals planning to intervene in the clients' social networks. Fourth, information about the *ethnic and cultural backgrounds* of older clients is central to successful service delivery. Finally, *knowledge about initiating relationships* with elderly clients will facilitate the reception of services by older clients.

Knowledge about the older population. As Chapter 3 suggests, background information about the elderly population is essential to providing services to individual older clients. This information includes general knowledge and theory about the elderly. For the initial contact with older clients, important knowledge includes information about how older clients expect professionals to respond to their requests for services and how older clients respond if their expectations are violated. In addition, it would be helpful to know how aged individuals respond to being approached by a service provider. For example, are elderly clients generally receptive to contacts by social workers or are they intimidated or repulsed by such contacts? Finally, knowledge about the general and specific needs of the elderly is mandated. This information, outlined in Chapter 3, will enhance the formation of relationships between service providers and clients.

Information about the specific client. Prior to the first contact with an older client, it is important to gain information about that individual when possible. Information about the elderly population as a whole is necessary; however, each client and the social systems with which they are involved vary somewhat from the average. Certain questions must be answered in order to approach an older client successfully. If a client has been referred for services by a third party, it is beneficial to request information about the client from the referral source. If the client requests services, some basic information can be requested at the time of the initial request.

Knowledge about the older client that is relevant at this stage in the service delivery process includes preliminary information concerning the following: (1) the client's presenting problems (i.e., what specific difficulties have caused the client to request services or to be referred for services); (2) when the presenting problems began and the length of their duration; (3) whether the client has experienced these problems in the past; (4) information about previous services the client has received from the service provider's agency or another social service agency; (5) what medication the client is currently taking; (6) the status of the client's physical condition; (7) the client's relationship to significant others, including family, friends, groups, and formal organizations; and (8) the client's expectations of the service delivery process. This information will be brief at the initial contact stage. However, preliminary information will aid the service provider during the data gathering stage.

Some of this information can be obtained informally from the client at the time services are requested. An older client calling for services would likely not expect a lengthy interview at this point, but the client can be engaged in a discussion that brings out the information needed at this stage. If a client is referred by another source, some of this information can be gathered from that source. If the client or a referral source is unable to provide the information needed, it may be helpful to request the client's permission to contact family members or others close to the client to gain this information. Specific skills utilized to obtain the knowledge needed about the individual client will be described under the Task section, below.

Knowledge about social systems. Chapters 2 and 3 deal with social systems and the interpersonal relationships of older clients. The relationships between older persons and others include helping relationships that can be supportive socially, physically, financially, or emotionally. Most older individuals have informal support systems, whether those systems are in the form of family or substitute family members (Shanas, 1979b). Older persons may also receive help from formal support systems.

Professionals who lack knowledge about their clients' social networks are limited in their ability to contribute to the problem solving process (Herr and Weakland, 1979). Service providers who have knowledge about the behavior of the elderly in relation to their social networks are at an advantage in terms of the questions that they can ask prior to or at the time of the initial interview. An assumption that older people are isolated from others prevents the worker from asking questions about resources that may be available to the client. In addition, not asking clients about significant others may indicate to clients that the service provider lacks interest in their lives. Conversely, beginning the initial interview by obtaining preliminary information about the client's environment, including internal and significant external social systems, indicates to clients that the service provider is concerned with all aspects of their lives. Also, asking clients about their relationships with others, about the help they receive and give and about their feelings can provide preliminary information about the client's functioning. The following case is an illustration of this.

Case Example 4.4

Miss Landers contacted a retirement village about the possibility of becoming a resident. She was given an appointment with a social worker employed by the facility. The administrator questioned Miss Landers about why she wanted to move to the village and Miss Landers responded that she needed increasing amounts of help in order to continue living in her own home. Thorough questioning revealed that she did receive a good deal of help from her two nephews and a cousin who lived near her. However, Miss Landers was concerned that she was imposing on these individuals and was uncomfortable in asking them to continue to help. Miss Landers stated that she currently was not receiving services from any formal helping agencies.

Miss Landers related that she and her cousin had a friendship that extended over the years. Also, she and her nephews had always been fond of one another. The administrator requested Miss Landers' permission to contact the relatives who had been involved in helping her in order to determine their feelings about meeting some of her needs. Miss Landers agreed to this and also gave the administrator permission to contact various social service agencies in the area to determine whether they had available resources that would allow her to remain in her own home. Miss Landers indicated that her wish was to stay in her home, but that she felt it was too much of an imposition on others.

As a result of contacting Miss Landers' nephews and cousin, it was discovered that they were unaware of her concerns about imposing on them. The administrator suggested a meeting with Miss Landers and her relatives in which each individual expressed his or her feelings regarding their relationship. It was agreed that if Miss Landers remained in her home, formal services would be needed. However, Miss Lander's relatives clearly stated their desire to share in caregiving and their feeling that she was not a unwanted burden to them.

Whether or not Miss Landers chooses to enter the retirement community, she experienced a beginning relationship with a professional who cared about more than one aspect of her life. The fact that the administrator requested information about others significant to Miss Landers and about Miss Landers' feelings allowed the client to feel the administrator's concern for her. If Miss Landers does enter the retirement community, she will have already begun a trusting relationship with the administrator. If she remains in her own home, the administrator will have strengthened the relationships that currently exist between Miss Landers and significant others, as well as possibly having established successful relationships between Miss Landers and formal resource systems.

In addition, the administrator's contacts with Miss Landers' family members at this time may help the administrator to relate to them in a positive manner in the future, should Miss Landers decide to enter the village. A knowledge that older clients have social networks and internal components allowed the administrator to begin intervention with the client system in a manner that contributes to client trust and to the future success of service delivery.

Knowledge about backgrounds of older clients. Another area of knowledge important to service providers is the ethnic and cultural setting in which the client functions or from which the client comes. If the older client is a member of a minority group, a practitioner requires accurate knowledge about the client's background. Faulty stereotypes exist concerning minority elderly. For example, Mindel (1983: 208) states

The Black family has been criticized as "sick" and "pathological," unable to care for its own and to produce productive, responsible members of society. An enormous amount of data and research in recent years has emerged to challenge this view. The kin group, it has been discovered, functions as a strong support system for its members, providing a whole range of services to family, frequently beyond the narrowly defined nuclear families of orientation and procreation.

Research findings also indicate that older black family members are frequently involved in caring for and helping other family members (Mindel, 1983). However, if a service provider subscribed to the belief that older black elderly come from dysfunctional families and are alienated from family members, their approach to an elderly black client could hinder their future relationship. The practitioner in Case Example 4.5 does not make this error.

Case Example 4.5

Mrs. Jackson, a 72-year-old black woman, was admitted to the community hospital following a heart attack. Prior to this, she had been physically active and involved with her family. For three years, Mrs. Jackson had lived with her granddaughter and had watched her granddaughter's children after school.

The hospital social worker, Mr. Baker, had visited Mrs. Jackson and gained information concerning her involvement with her granddaughter's family and her desire to continue active involvement with them. He had also talked with her granddaughter and discovered that the granddaughter wished for Mrs. Jackson to return to her home. Mrs. Baker's physician suggested that when she was ready to leave the hospital, Mrs. Baker be discharged to a nursing facility so that she would not be a burden to her granddaughter. The social worker was prepared with information about Mrs. Baker and her relationship to her family. He was aware that both she and her granddaughter depended on one another.

The granddaughter had contacted neighbors who agreed to check on Mrs. Baker during the day. In addition, Mrs. Baker could be there when her grandchildren came home from school and they could provide support for one another. The social worker advocated for this plan, as he felt that it was crucial to Mrs. Baker's emotional well-being. The physician agreed to this.

In the course of follow-up, the social worker found that upon recuperating, Mrs. Baker had happily resumed many of the household tasks that she had carried out prior to her illness.

If the medical social worker, in Case Example 4.5, had lacked knowledge about older black families, he might have assumed that his client, Mrs. Baker, did not have involvement in a reciprocal family support system. He could have agreed with the physician's assumption that Mrs. Baker was a burden rather than a help to her granddaughter. Had the physician's recommendation been carried out, Mrs. Baker would have been denied the opportunity to have her contributory needs met. In addition, she would have had less control over her environment had she been placed in a nursing facility rather than in her granddaughter's home, where she clearly wanted to go. Knowledge about the client's background during the initial phase of service delivery allowed a service plan to be developed that met the needs of the older client.

Older clients' religious orientations *may* be closely tied to their ethnic backgrounds. This is not always the case; however, information concerning this benefits the delivery of services. Lack of knowledge about an older client's religious orientation may result in obstacles to initiating a relationship with an older client, as the following case example illustrates.

Case Example 4.6

Mrs. Herr was an elderly resident in a midwestern long-term care facility. She had entered the facility after living with her daughter's family for several years. Until moving to her daughter's home, Mrs. Herr had lived in Pennsylvania all of her life. Her background was Pennsylvania Dutch.

The social worker at the long-term care facility met with Mrs. Herr soon after her admission. The social worker, in an attempt to make Mrs. Herr feel more comfortable at the facility, told Mrs. Herr about an upcoming dance at the facility and about a jewelry making class which was to begin soon. Mrs. Herr did not show any interest in either of these activities and became very quiet. Because of this, the social worker felt that Mrs. Herr was not interested in talking to her at that time. She decided to approach Mrs. Herr at a later time. In addition, she did not present information about other activities available in the facility.

It was during a conversation with Mrs. Herr's daughter that the worker discovered that Mrs. Herr was a Mennonite and that her belief system precluded dancing and wearing jewelry. The daughter related to the social worker that her mother had been feeling very lonely at the facility and that she would like to talk to the social worker again and to attend other activities that did not violate her beliefs.

Had the social worker begun her relationship with Mrs. Herr with knowledge about the client's religious affiliation, she might have prevented Mrs. Herr's feelings of loneliness. In addition, she might have been able to establish a more trusting relationship with Mrs. Herr as well as have suggested activities that were compatible with the client's interests.

Knowledge about initiating relationships with older clients. During the initial phase, it is necessary to have knowledge about how to approach older clients and/or their significant social systems, as well as how to respond when approached. As discussed, it is helpful to have information about the specific client prior to the first contact, when possible. This information allows the human service worker to tailor an approach that is best suited to the individual client. The worker may not have prior information, as the first indication that a client requires services may come when the client initiates a contact. With or without prior information, the worker benefits from knowledge about how to (1) listen to the client, (2) clearly respond to the client's spoken and unspoken concerns, (3) discuss both the client's and worker's expectations of their roles, and (4) obtain the information necessary to accomplish this.

Other knowledge helpful in approaching older clients includes an awareness that older clients respond most positively to service providers when addressed by their formal names, rather than by their first names. In working with older clients, it has been my observation that clients resent being called "Mary" as opposed to being called "Mrs. Smith." This is particularly true when the service provider is years younger than the client. It may appear to older clients that providers are being impertinent when clients are not addressed formally. If professionals wish to call clients by their first names, clients should first be asked how they prefer to be addressed.

It is also valuable at this stage to know that older clients do sometimes resist services and to be able to recognize client resistance when it occurs. One stereotype of the elderly is that they are outspoken and cantankerous. As a result of this stereotype, it might be assumed that older people will clearly let a practitioner know if the services offered are not wanted or present a problem. However, each elderly client is a unique individual and many elderly will not openly discuss their lack of interest with the service provider although, as Weeks (1983) notes, they may be disinterested. Resistance may be shown in indirect ways. It is important for the worker to be sensitive to this and to encourage clients to express their own views of the services to be offered.

Also, knowledge about the expectations of older clients is necessary in initiating relationships. Fischer (1978) has stated that significant numbers of clients end their relationships with case-workers after the initial contact due to unfulfilled expectations about what would occur during that contact with the service provider. He cites research revealing that "20 to 60 percent of our clients drop out of treatment after the first interview" and suggests that "one of the major factors that appears related to those high rates of discontinuance involves clients' expectations of treatment, particularly a lack of congruence between caseworker and client in the ways they perceive the client's problems and how to handle them" (Fischer, 1978: 140).

Research indicates that "continuance in the professional relation-ship can be increased, and/or positively enhanced, when the initial contacts with the client are devoted to structuring the mutual expectations of client and practitioner" (Fischer, 1978: 140). This information supports propositions of exchange theorists who suggest that individuals engaged in relationships that do not meet their expectations will withdraw from those relationships (Thibault and Kelly, 1959) or do damage to them (Blau, 1964), while individuals receiving something from a relationship that they view as positive will stay involved in that reciprocal relationship (Gouldner, 1960). Unger and Powell note that social networks "are characterized by reciprocity" and that reciprocal relationships aid the functioning of social networks. "If the process of exchanging aid with network members becomes aversive . . . a person may forfeit the use of the network" (1980: 571). Therefore, clients whose expectations are met are more likely to remain involved in a productive relationship with service providers.

Although the research cited above refers to general client populations, the elderly also hold expectations for relationships in which they are involved; and the morale of the elderly is negatively affected when their expectations are violated (Seelbach and Sauer, 1977). For service providers planning to become a part of the elderly client's social network, an awareness that the elderly client has expectations of the professional relationship and that those expectations can be violated would be helpful. Therefore, obtaining information about the expectations of specific clients is necessary.

TASKS

The values, purpose, and knowledge of the geriatric service provider lead to tasks that are planned and carried out in practice. During the initial contact stage, service provision benefits from the establishment of tasks. Clearly established general tasks enable the service provider to potentially contribute to a relationship that will facilitate service delivery.

At the initial stage of working with an older client, the tasks that flow from the service provider's values, purpose, and knowledge include (1) *preparation* for the first client contact; (2) *application* of values, purpose, and knowledge; and (3) the *application of skills* developed for work with older clients. These tasks are relevant for work with individual elderly clients, with older client groups and/or with social systems with which the client is or may become involved. The following case examples and discussions deal with the tasks helpful for practice with the elderly.

Preparation for the initial interview is vital to its success. Fischer (1978) stresses the necessity of planning for work with clients. Compton and Galaway suggest that preparation is the "first task" of the "initial contact" (1979: 279). Case Example 4.7 deals with the issue of preparation in the formation of a group for spouses of elderly clients. In this case, the counselor knew his clients and their families prior to becoming involved with them in a group setting, but has formed an initial relationship with them as group members.

Case Example 4.7

Robert Alexander is a counselor employed by a long-term care facility. For some time, he has felt that families of elderly residents could benefit from having the opportunity to talk with one another in order to share concerns.

As a result, he decided to begin a support group for some of the families of residents in his facility. He began by researching the literature on groups with families of the elderly and on stresses and needs experienced by families who have elderly members residing in long-term care facilities. In addition, he reviewed case records to determine needs that had been expressed by families in his interviews with them and in their conversations with other staff members.

Utilizing this background information, he decided that spouses of elderly residents could benefit from a group focused on stresses they experience in living without their partners. He contacted spouses who had indicated to him or to other staff that this was a stressful area to them and whom he felt would participate in and benefit from the group experience.

Although Mr. Alexander already had formed a relationship with the spouses of the residents, he was initiating a relationship with a group of individuals. That relationship would take a slightly different form than the relationship that he previously had with each group member. In contacting the spouses, Mr. Alexander informed each of his desire to establish a group, described the function and focus of the group and asked if they would be interested. He approached each spouse based on his knowledge of that individual and his or her interests and needs, giving information to each that was appropriate to their concerns. As a result of Mr. Alexander's research on forming groups and his knowledge about the needs of each of the spouses, several spouses joined and continued in the group led by Mr. Alexander.

In this case, the counselor initiated a contact with the spouses of residents based on his experience with them and on information provided about them by other staff members of the long-term care facility. In addition, he focused group goals on issues of interest to the spouses. He also began this stage with knowledge about groups with family members of the elderly and with knowledge about the problems experienced by older families. His preparation, development of a knowledge base, and skill in contacting the spouses contributed to the success of the group. The two cases that follow also emphasize preparation for the initial stage of the relationship as well as the importance of *applying values, purpose, and knowledge and skills to work with older clients* in this stage.

In Case Example 4.8, the social worker has the responsibility of initiating a relationship with an individual who is already receiving services from another professional. The client has shown a sudden change in behavior, and the professional working with him has requested that the social worker become involved for assessment purposes. Again, the social worker prepared for her initial contact with the client by reviewing information concerning the client's problem as well as gathering background information on the client himself from appropriate individuals. In addition, the social worker utilized skills appropriate to the client's situation in order to initiate contact with the client.

Case Example 4.8

Mr. Taylor had received services from the local visiting nurse organization for several months. The services had been provided so that he could remain in his own home rather than move to a nursing facility. Mr. Taylor was a diabetic and had sores on his feet that would not heal. He needed daily care for these. In addition, he required injections for diabetes and medication for several other chronic ailments. Over the months, Mr. Taylor had expressed his appreciation for the aid that the nurse provided. He and the nurse who visited his home had developed a positive relationship. However, Mr. Taylor had recently become withdrawn when the nurse visited him. Finally, he stopped responding to her at all when she entered his home. It appeared to the nurse that Mr. Taylor was eating meals and caring for his basic needs only sporadically.

The nurse talked with her supervisor and they met with the social worker, Mrs. Simpson, a consultant with the visiting nurse organization. The social worker agreed to meet with Mr. Taylor for the purpose of determining the reasons behind his behavior toward the visiting nurse. Prior to meeting with Mr. Taylor, Mrs. Simpson reviewed the medical and social information available in the nursing files concerning him. In addition, Mrs. Simpson spoke with the nurse who had been providing services to Mr. Taylor for the past several months. From these two sources, Mrs. Simpson discovered that Mr. Taylor lived alone (his wife had died about six months earlier), and he had two adult, married children, a son and daughter, living nearby and several adolescent grandchildren. The chart revealed that Mr. Taylor had a close relationship with his daughter, but that he seldom saw his son. The daughter did housework for Mr. Taylor and also shopped for his groceries. His oldest grandson mowed his lawn and did weeding for him. The chart also indicated that Mr. Taylor had been hospitalized soon after his wife's death because he had stopped eating. Following hospitalization, he had returned home and had eaten regular meals, which he prepared himself.

Following a review of Mr. Taylor's chart and a meeting with the nurse, Mrs. Simpson reviewed information on depression in the elderly, organic brain syndrome, and older family relationships. Because Mr. Taylor had not been seen by a physician since his behavior had changed, Mrs. Simpson suggested that the nursing organization refer him for a medical examination. She also requested the visiting nurse to tell Mr. Taylor that she had asked the social worker to visit him and to establish a time when that would be convenient for Mr. Taylor. Mrs. Simpson's conversation with Mr. Taylor was as follows:

> MRS. SIMPSON: Mr. Taylor, the nurse who has been visiting you for the last few months has asked me to meet with you. She said that this would be a good time for me to come. Are you free right now?
>
> MR. TAYLOR: I don't know.
>
> MRS. SIMPSON: Well, why don't I just stay for a few minutes today, and maybe I can come back another time that's more convenient for you.
>
> MR. TAYLOR: Um.
>
> MRS. SIMPSON: Did the nurse tell you why she wanted me to visit you?
>
> MR. TAYLOR: I'm not sure.
>
> MRS. SIMPSON: She asked me to meet with you because she's concerned that you haven't been taking your medication or eating lately. She's worried about your health.
>
> MR. TAYLOR: I'm doing okay. I eat what I need.
>
> MRS. SIMPSON: Have you felt well recently?
>
> MR. TAYLOR: Oh, I've been okay.
>
> MRS. SIMPSON: You saw your doctor recently, didn't you?
>
> MR. TAYLOR: The doctor says I'm pretty healthy except that I need to gain some weight. He says if I don't, he'll have to put me in the hospital.
>
> MRS. SIMPSON: The doctor says you might have to go to the hospital?
>
> MR. TAYLOR: Yeah, to get my weight up. It's down from where it should be. But I don't want to go, I've been in that hospital before and it's no good.
>
> MRS. SIMPSON: Before I came to see you, I talked with your nurse and she said that you had been hospitalized before. You didn't like that?
>
> MR. TAYLOR: Nope. I won't go back.
>
> MRS. SIMPSON: How long ago were you there?
>
> MR. TAYLOR: About six months ago. I won't go back.
>
> MRS. SIMPSON: You didn't like it there.
>
> MR. TAYLOR: Are you here to get me to go to the hospital?

MRS. SIMPSON: No, I'm not. In fact, one of the main reasons that I'm here is because your nurse wants you to be able to stay at home and she thought that if the three of us worked together, we might be able to make that happen.

MR. TAYLOR: What do you mean?

MRS. SIMPSON: Well, if we look at the things that are keeping you from weighing what you should, or from eating what you need to weigh enough, maybe we can help you to work toward getting your weight up to where it should be so that you can stay at home.

MR. TAYLOR: I want to stay at home.

MRS. SIMPSON: I know that you do. Mr. Taylor, it would help us if I had more information about your situation than your nurse can give me. Could you and I meet tomorrow and talk again?

MR. TAYLOR: Yes, I'd like that.

MRS. SIMPSON: Would you be willing for me to talk with your daughter to see if she has any information that would help us?

MR. TAYLOR: Okay, but not my son.

MRS. SIMPSON: I won't talk with anyone other than the visiting nurse organization without your permission. I want you to know that the things we talk about will be not be shared with other people, unless there is a serious concern for your health, and then I would need to talk with your doctor or nurse. Otherwise, I will not share information without your permission.

MR. TAYLOR: Um.

MRS. SIMPSON: Could we plan to meet again at 2:00 tomorrow?

MR. TAYLOR: I'd like that.

The tasks that Mrs. Simpson needed to carry out during this initial contact with Mr. Taylor included gathering background information on Mr. Taylor's problem *(preparation for the interview)*, gaining his trust, maintaining objectivity, and involving Mr. Taylor as a participant for the purpose of establishing a relationship with him *(application of values and purpose)*. A relationship was necessary for Mrs. Simpson to assess Mr. Taylor's situation so that appropriate services could be provided to him, and Mrs. Simpson's *skill* in developing this was vital.

The background information that Mrs. Simpson reviewed indicated that a depressed older person may display symptoms that can be confused with organic brain syndrome (Butler and Lewis, 1983). Mr. Taylor's nurse had questioned whether his behavior was a symptom of organic brain syndrome. However, the literature reviewed by the social worker indicated that signs of depression include some of the symptoms that Mr. Taylor had exhibited, such as a decreased appetite, and listlessness (Wantz and Gay, 1981). It was important that Mrs. Simpson not approach Mr. Taylor with the assumption that he was suffering from organic brain syndrome rather than depression. It was also necessary not to assume that Mr. Taylor was depressed, since the characteristics he was revealing can also be signs of other illnesses (Weeks, 1984). For this reason, Mrs. Simpson asked for a physical examination prior to her interview.

Gaining Mr. Taylor's trust was somewhat difficult because of his concerns about hospitalization. In addition, his withdrawal prevented him from reaching out to Mrs. Simpson. Mrs. Simpson facilitated Mr. Taylor's ability to trust her by asking the nurse, with whom he had a good relationship, to set up her visit with him. As Pincus and Minahan (1973) note, resistance to a professional may be lessened by having a party whom the client trusts first contact the client.

Upon approaching Mr. Taylor, Mrs. Simpson let him slowly adjust to her presence. She recognized how difficult it can be for anyone to receive professional help (Compton and Galaway, 1979). She did not bombard him with questions nor did she overwhelm him with information. Instead, she stated that she would only stay for several minutes, which she did. She also explained clearly why she had come to see him (telling him that his nurse had asked her to come and that the nurse is concerned about him) and let him know that the information she had about him had come from his nurse, whom he trusted. Throughout the interview, Mrs. Simpson allowed Mr. Taylor to meet the need of maintaining some control over the relationship. As a result of her responses, she enhanced Mr. Taylor's trust.

Trust was also gained by clarifying expectations. Mrs. Simpson gave a clear description of what she hoped would happen: "one of the main reasons that I am here is because your nurse wants you to be able to stay at home and she thought that if the three of us worked together, we might be able to make that happen." At this point, Mrs. Simpson conveyed her expectation that Mr. Taylor could cope with his situation. Since the need to cope is basic, this expectation is a reassuring one. At a later date, when Mr. Taylor could handle more information, it would be necessary for Mrs. Simpson to clarify Mr. Taylor's and her role expectations to an even greater extent. As Fischer (1978) notes, both the worker's and the client's role expectations should be clearly defined. However, at this point, the amount of information provided was appropriate for Mr. Taylor. As part of clarifying her expectations of what their relationship would lead to, Mrs. Simpson did not promise Mr. Taylor things that she could not fulfill. For example, she did not tell him that he could remain at home.

Mrs. Simpson also indicated her expectation that Mr. Taylor would be an active participant in their relationship through her use of reflection. She did not tell Mr. Taylor what she thought he was feeling, but reflected his feelings. In this way, she showed that she understood what was important to him (Okun, 1982) as well as let him know that his thoughts were important to her. Through this, Mr. Taylor's need to contribute to the relationship was met to a small extent. As a result of Mrs. Simpson's resposes to Mr. Taylor, she has begun to form a linkage with him. Consequently, she is a potential source of external energy for Mr. Taylor.

Utilization of skills. Service providers will want to apply specific skills to tasks carried out during the initial stage. The skills required at this stage involve the following: (1) responding directly to the client's concerns; (2) gaining information by questioning the client in a supportive manner; (3) probing without offending the client; (4) listening and responding objectively; (5) validating the client's feelings; and (6) clarifying expectations. These skills are illustrated in the following case example.

In Case Example 4.9 a human service worker has begun a relationship with the family member of an elderly person. The worker has come to this interview prepared with knowledge about how to respond to an approach by the adult child of an elderly person and *skills that actualize that knowledge.*

Case Example 4.9

Mrs. Jansen, an adult service worker for the county welfare department, was contacted by Miss Hadley about Miss Hadley's elderly mother. Miss Hadley telephoned Mrs. Jansen to request information about available community services that could help her mother remain in her own home.

MISS HADLEY: I wondered if you could tell me something about how I could help my mother. She needs help during the day and I'm unable to be there for her because I work.

MRS. JANSEN: Could you tell me a little more about the type of help your mother needs?

MISS HADLEY: Well, she can't cook for himself, even though she tries to, and she gets bored during the daytime and calls me at work asking me to come home.

MRS. JANSEN: Your mother can't cook for herself?

MISS HADLEY: No she can't. She turns on the burners and forgets to turn them off. I'm worried that she'll set the house on fire. And sometimes she forgets to eat at all. I hate to think that she goes from breakfast to dinner without food, but I can't get home at noon.

MRS. JANSEN: Can you tell me how long this has been a problem?

MISS HADLEY: Well, I guess for several months. I've done everything that I can think of, but I'm at my wits' end.

MRS. JANSEN: Could you tell me something about the things you have done to solve the problem?

MISS HADLEY: Well, I've taken sick days at work, but I can't keep doing that. I've asked neighbors to check on her, but that's too much to ask over a long period of time. I've thought of having her go to a nursing home, but I don't want to do that. I feel so helpless.

MRS. JANSEN: It sounds as though you've tried a lot of things, but that it's been frustrating.

MISS HADLEY: It certainly has. Is there any way you could help me?

MRS. JANSEN: Let me outline some things that our agency does. First, though, I need a little more information about your mother so that I can tell you the services that might be most appropriate. How old is your mother?

MISS HADLEY: She's 80.

MRS. JANSEN: Does your mother live with you in your home?

MISS HADLEY: We live together. It's her house, though. I came back home several years ago after my father died.

MISS JANSEN: How long has it been since your mother had a physical examination?

MISS HADLEY: Probably a year ago. Do you think that she's sick?

MISS JANSEN: No, I don't know that. I ask that question because sometimes an elderly person's ability to function is influenced by health. Also, medication can affect an older person's ability to do things. Is your mother currently taking medication?

MISS HADLEY: No, she's not.

MISS JANSEN: You mentioned that you moved in with your mother after your father died several years ago. What happened that led you to return home?

MISS HADLEY: I guess I went home because my mother was so lonely after my father died and I thought it would help if I moved in. I lived nearby, anyway, and was spending so much time at home that it seemed easier to move in.

MRS. JANSEN: It sounds as though you have been involved in helping your mother for some time. Is anyone else available to help you provide support to your mother?

MISS HADLEY: No. I'm the only child and we don't have any other relatives living near to us. My mother has many friends, but they're elderly, too. I have friends who would be glad to help if they knew how I feel, but I'm really not comfortable asking people to help me.

MRS. JANSEN: You must feel really overwhelmed at times. What you're going through happens sometimes when there is only one person available to care for an elderly parent. There is a range of services available for people who are in your mother's situation. Programs exist that provide a small amount of help, like having warm meals brought in at noontime, to more extensive aids, such as programs where older people receive care during the day outside of the home and then return home in the evening. I would like to meet with both you and your mother so that we could discuss this and determine whether either of you would like to try some of the services that are available.

Mrs. Jansen began the interview by *responding directly to her client's concerns.* She requested Miss Hadley to further clarify her initial statement so that she could better understand her request. This approach is much more helpful than trying to guess what the client is requesting or making assumptions about the client's request. Had Mrs. Jansen responded to Miss Hadley's first statement with, "I would be glad to put you into contact with some long-term care facilities," she would likely have alienated Miss Hadley, since a nursing home placement for her mother was specifically what Miss Hadley did not want.

Each of Mrs. Jansen's responses at the beginning of the interview involved questioning Miss Hadley in order to *gain more informa-tion.* This questioning was done in a way that was supportive of Miss Hadley and *that communicated Mrs. Jansen's concern about Miss Hadley's situation.* As a result, Miss Hadley provided some information to which Mrs. Jansen could immediately respond and some information that called for a response at a later time. For example, when the relationship is more firmly established, Mrs. Jansen might want to seek more information about the quality of the relationship between Miss Hadley and her mother. This information could facilitate the delivery of services.

When children of an elderly client approach a service provider, it is often after they have tried every informal avenue of problem solving available to them. To approach a professional about an older parent may symbolize to the children that they have failed in caring for their parents. The professional who does not listen carefully to the adult child's concerns or who attaches her own meanings to the child's concerns can add to the frustration or guilt that the child *may* be experiencing. Mrs. Jansen was able to *remain objective* and respond in a manner that indicated that she was hearing the concerns that Miss Hadley was feeling and expressing. Through this, Miss Hadley was able to clarify her concerns for herself as well as for her mother, and future problem solving was enhanced.

Mrs. Jansen also facilitated the professional relationship by verbally showing that she recognized what Miss Hadley had been through in attempting to care for her mother: "It sounds as though you've tried a lot of things, but that it's been frustrating." Later, she responded by saying, "You must feel really overwhelmed at times." In stating this, Mrs. Jansen acknowledged that Miss Hadley had cared about and for her mother and also *validated Miss Hadley's feeling of frustration.*

When Miss Hadley asked how Mrs. Jansen could help her, the social worker *responded directly* by saying that services were available, but that she would need more information. Mrs. Jansen gained helpful information about Miss Hadley's and her mother's interactions with others that could be expanded on and dealt with at a later date. When she had obtained the information that she needed at that point, Mrs. Jansen described the range of services that were available to elderly persons in Miss Hadley's mother's situation. She indicated that she *expected both Miss Hadley and her mother to be participants* in the process of choosing services and established an appointment with them for that purpose.

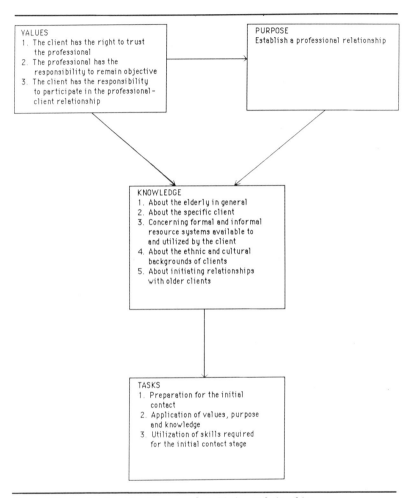

VALUES
1. The client has the right to trust the professional
2. The professional has the responsibility to remain objective
3. The client has the responsibility to participate in the professional-client relationship

PURPOSE
Establish a professional relationship

KNOWLEDGE
1. About the elderly in general
2. About the specific client
3. Concerning formal and informal resource systems available to and utilized by the client
4. About the ethnic and cultural backgrounds of clients
5. About initiating relationships with older clients

TASKS
1. Preparation for the initial contact
2. Application of values, purpose and knowledge
3. Utilization of skills required for the initial contact stage

Figure 4.1: Service Provision Framework: Initiating Relationships

CONCLUSION

As illustrated in Figure 4.1, the values emphasized by the service provider during the initial contact stage influence the purpose for contact with the older client. Both values and purpose will have an impact on knowledge gained and utilized, which in turn guides the tasks enacted by the service provider. In the initial contact stage, the human service worker will subscribe to the following values: (1) the client's right to place trust in the worker; (2) the importance of remaining objective; and (3) the client's responsibility to participate in the professional-client relationship.

The purpose of the initial contact is to establish a relationship characterized by professionalism. If this is accomplished, the older client may become more accepting of the external sources of energy the professional can make available in this and later stages.

During this phase, the service provider requires knowledge concerning (1) older individuals in general, (2) the specific client, (3) formal and informal resource systems available to and utilized by the older client, and (4) initiating relationships.

The professional's values, purpose, and knowledge direct the tasks carried out at this stage. As a result, the professional will prepare for the initial contact, apply values, purpose, and knowledge to work with the older client and develop skills to enhance the professional relationship.

Through the initiation of a professional relationship with older clients, the service provider develops linkages with clients and relevant others. A positive beginning will help older clients as they make the adjustments necessary to meet internal and external goals. The service provider begins to gain information that will permit resources to be obtained to meet clients' needs. In this way, clients' environments also adjust, enhancing clients' abilities to meet internal and external goals. Throughout the initial relationship, the professional provides energy to the client by meeting basic needs to control, be expressive, contribute, and exert influence over the relationship.

5

GATHERING DATA

At the data gathering stage, the provider attempts to pull together all the pertinent information relative to the client's situation and presenting problems. Throughout the elderly client-service provider relationship, however, additional information will present itself. As a result, gathering information about the elderly client is an ongoing process (Fischer, 1978). It begins with the initial interview and continues throughout the relationship. Although the client has presented the reason for seeking the professional's services during the initial contact stage and preliminary information has been obtained, additional knowledge about the client and the client's situation is necessary before service priorities are established and needs met.

Determining the older client's situation is more involved than gathering information about other age groups. "Not only has the older client brought to old age the accumulated experiences of a lifetime which influence his present behavior, but current functional problems and other closely related ones susceptible to rapid intersystemic changes" (Silverstone and Burack-Weiss, 1983: 11-12). However, as with other age groups, the data gathering stage involves relying on values, striving toward a purpose, and applying knowledge through skills.

VALUES

The data gathering stage provides the professional with the opportunity to employ two basic values of the service delivery process: treating the client with *respect* and promoting client *contributions* to the service delivery process. Respect for the client at this stage involves (1) providing a clear description of the data gathering process, (2) explaining and maintaining confidentiality, and (3) accurately probing for information. When clients are respected during this phase of the process, they will be allowed to *contribute* through informed consent and through providing their view of the situation. In addition, they will have some *control* over what becomes of the information that the practitioner has about them and how that information is utilized.

Respecting the older client. Clients are shown respect during this stage of the process when *the reasons for requesting information are clearly explained.* Respecting clients in this way serves to reassure the older client. For older clients who are unsure about their futures or for those who have had little control over the plans that have been made for them, another unknown person requesting information can have many meanings. It is beneficial to provide clients with an explicit explanation about *why* the information in regard to them is needed and *what will be done with that information.* This prevents clients from making false and possibly frightening assumptions. In addition, this validates the older client's worth as an individual.

When the client is aware of the reasons for being questioned, he or she will be more willing to provide the needed information. In addition, the client is more likely to allow boundaries to be opened and to accept the support and resources (external energy) that the worker may provide at this and later stages. Consequently, setting priorities and delivering services will be positively influenced through clear and precise explanations.

An explanation of *confidentiality* and its limits also exemplifies respect for the older client. Following a discussion of the reasons for requesting information concerning the elderly client, confidentiality should be explained. Elderly clients have the right to the assurance and maintenance of confidentiality about information concerning them. This involves telling clients if other individuals in the agency will have access to the professional's records. Clients should also be told that information concerning them will not be provided to any other individual or agency without their permission.

Accurate probing ensures that questions will be asked and discussions guided in a sensitive, thorough manner. Older clients have the right to be questioned in a manner that does not deny their dignity. Accurate probing implies that the information gained about the client (and utilized to determine service priorities and interventions) is complete and correct. The questioning that is done by the service provider must be thorough and lead to realistic knowledge about the client. If not, services offered may not only be inappropriate but could do damage to the client and others involved with him or her.

The material gathered through accurate probing should be integrated in a realistic manner. As with any data gathering process, the information is obtained to determine the realities of the situation. This allows the client to be viewed more accurately than when materials are gathered to support the views of the professional.

The human service worker *promotes the older client's contributions* through involving the client in providing information that will facilitate meeting the client's needs. Only when individuals feel competent to contribute to meeting their own needs can they begin to contribute to others. The service provider should request the involvement of those older individuals who are capable of contributing.

PURPOSE

The professional's purpose at this stage is to gather enough information so that problems can be accurately determined and resources matched to need in later stages of the service delivery process. Fischer (1978: 249) has stated the purpose of this stage is to gain "detailed information about the problem situation that will lead directly to the establishing of interventive goals, a strategy of intervention, and selection of specific procedures of intervention."

Consequently, the data gathering process exists for a purpose—to contribute to meeting client's needs—and not only to develop an understanding of the client's situation (Fischer, 1978). Understanding the interrelationships of the older client's sub- and suprasystems is necessary *because* it provides the understanding necessary for useful intervention.

KNOWLEDGE

The knowledge required by the service provider at the data gathering stage includes knowledge about (1) the *coping patterns and needs* of older individuals; (2) *utilization of the social systems approach* in obtaining data; (3) *how and when to seek information* from professionals from other disciplines; and (4) *specific questions to ask older clients and other sources of information.*

Knowledge about coping patterns and needs of older individuals. The information presented in Chapter 3 is vital to the service provider working with aged clients. Knowledge concerning the elderly and their needs enables the practitioner to distinguish between old age and illness and to ask appropriate questions concerning each. A lack of knowledge about the aging process can lead the professional to assume that certain illnesses and behaviors are characteristic of the elderly rather than to seek information about how older persons can be helped to overcome their problems. An assumption that the elderly client's problems are the result of old age can maintain those problems. Knowledge about the elderly allows professionals to gain information leading to change and to provide the older client with hope when appropriate.

In addition to individualized needs that the older client might be experiencing, the basic needs of elderly clients at this stage are several. First, the client has the need to *cope* by continuing adjustment to the relationship with the practitioner. Second, the client has the need to be *expressive*. As noted above, this is met during the data gathering stage through soliciting information from the client and validating the importance of the information that the client provides. Third, the older client has the need to *achieve some control over the relationship* with the service provider. Several ways in which this can be achieved have been discussed under the "Values" section of this chapter. Other methods of accomplishing this will be explicated in the "Tasks" section, below. Finally, the older client needs to feel some ability to *contribute* to others. This can begin by encouraging clients to become active participants in meeting their own needs through supplying information about their situation.

Knowledge regarding utilization of the social systems approach. Knowledge about use of the social systems approach is required when obtaining information from and about older clients. When the social systems approach is applied at the data gathering stage, it can be used during later phases of the service delivery process as well. The older client is a social system. The practitioner must gather information about the internal systems of the older client as well as systems external to the older client. Consequently, the practitioner will ask questions about the intellectual, psychological, physical, and spiritual (if appropriate) functioning of the older person. In addition, the practitioner will ask about the financial, social, housing, and other external factors that have an influence on his or her older client.

An awareness that *behavior does not have one, but many causes* is mandated. As Case Example 5.1, below, reveals, the service provider would be prevented from gaining necessary information if she assumed that an older client's problems could all be attributed to the one factor.

Case Example 5.1

Mrs. Jordan, a homemaker-home health aide supervisor was asked to meet with one of her aide's clients concerning a problem the aide was having in the client's home. The aide, who had only worked in Mr. Thompson's home for two weeks, had reported that he made sexual advances toward her when she was in his home and called her by another name when this occurred.

Mrs. Jordan met with Mr. Thompson and discovered that the name he called the aide was that of his deceased wife. His wife had died two years earlier. Mrs. Jordan decided that Mr. Thompson's behavior was the result of grieving for his wife and referred him to a group for elders who have lost their spouses.

Fortunately, the group leader asked both Mr. Thompson and his family for information and also referred him to his physician for a physical examination. The family reported that Mr. Thompson had been confused about with whom he was talking and where he was for the past three years. This had become more of a concern in the last year since he had moved to a new neighborhood. Lately, he had been found wandering around the neighborhood. The physician reported to the group leader that he believed Mr. Thompson had Alzheimer's disease. In addition, Mr. Thompson had several other health problems that required medication.

The practitioner can request information about interaction between subsystems and how clients interact with others in their environments. This provides knowledge about how clients gain and receive energy from internal and external sources, whether organization is sufficient to utilize the energy received, and the adjustment of clients to their current situations. This information will be utilized as the professional attempts to assess the problem and establish service priorities with clients.

Knowledge about initiating interactions with other professionals. When should a service provider contact other professionals from other disciplines? Certainly use of the social systems approach gives the provider an awareness of the various problems that exist and of the other professionals who are also involved with the client. This provides direction to seek information from others who specialize in those problem areas and from those who have contact with the client. For example, knowledge that a depressed older client is taking several types of medication would lead a social worker to contact a physician and request information about whether the interactions of those medications could contribute to depression. In another situation, a hospital discharge planner facilitating the discharge of an elderly hospital patient would want to speak with that patient's physician and with the hospital nursing staff to determine the level of the patient's functioning and their recommendations. The discharge planner would also want to talk with professionals in the community who had contact with the patient prior to hospitalization to gather information from those sources.

Knowledge about specific questions to ask. The service provider requires knowledge about specific areas in which to question the older client and/or relevant others. The Data Gathering Format presented here (in the Appendix to this chapter) indicates the areas that should be covered during the data gathering stage. The service provider's employing agency will frequently supply a format for gathering information regarding clients. The Data Gathering Format presented here provides human service professionals with questions that can expand the information they will gain from older clients and that will allow for an assessment of the older client's situation from a social systems perspective.

As shown in Case 5.2, under the "Tasks" section of this chapter, questioning will follow the flow of conversation to some extent in order to make the client more comfortable and to obtain a maximum amount of information. Consequently, the questions will not always be asked in the order listed. In addition, some questions may not be answered in one interview. When this is the case, the service provider can request information missed in later meetings with the client.

The Data Gathering Format outlines basic areas and issues to be covered. However, the service provider's questioning is not limited to these areas. Frequently, the client or other resource persons' responses will lead to further questioning on a topic or will point to an area that, for that client, has not been adequately covered. The information gained will alert the practitioner to whether other professionals, relatives, or friends of the client should be contacted for more information.

TASKS

The tasks that the service provider will carry out in the data gathering phase reflect the values, purpose, and knowledge of this stage. First, the service provider will attempt to make the client *comfortable with the questioning* that will take place. The second task will involve *appropriately gaining accurate information* concerning the client or other referral source's reasons for seeking the service provider and background information about the client and the client's situation.

Enhancing the client's comfort. The older client will feel more comfortable during the data collection stage when the professional provides information about what will occur and describes the limits of confidentiality. The professional is also responsible to take action so that confidentiality will be kept.

Confidentiality is maintained by meeting with the client in a private setting. For an older, frail client in an intergenerational household or an institutional setting, this may be difficult. However, it is important to ask other family members for privacy or, in an institutional setting, to arrange to see the client when the roommate and other staff will be out of the room. In addition, conversations about the client, such as telephone discussions requesting information about the client, made with the client's permission, should be completed out of the hearing of other staff and residents. This may not always be possible, as a bedridden client may share a room with another individual, also confined to bed. When this occurs, speaking quietly with the client may be the only alternative. In another situation, a family member may refuse to leave the room. Explaining why privacy is desired may help a family member to grant that by leaving. However if this does not occur, requesting privacy and attempting to gain it provide older clients with the message that the service provider views them as having dignity. When others are present, it would be important that the service provider not discuss information of an intimate nature unless the client indicates a wish to do so.

The written record of the data gathered should be stored in a place that will keep the client's confidence. The Federal Privacy Act of 1974 mandates that federal agencies maintain "physical safeguards" to ensure the confidentiality of records. Wilson (1978) suggests that records be kept in a locked storage unit, not left in the open to be seen by other clients or staff, and never taken home. For service providers in an institutional setting, this is impossible, of course. Physicians, nursing staff, and social service "share" a client's chart and each adds their notations to it. These charts, however, can be kept confidential from other residents and family members through safeguarding. The written summary concerning the client should not include conversations that would lessen the client's dignity. The following example, taken from an elderly long-term care resident's chart, does not accomplish this.

Mr. J. was admitted from the hospital on this date. He is a living vegetable. Permanent residency is suggested.

Wilson (1978: 37-39) suggests that confidentiality is enchanced when the following information is not included as part of the written record: (1) personal information about the client (e.g., intimate details or information about religious or political orientations) that are not pertinent to the service delivery process; (2) information of a "gossipy" nature (such as information provided by other clients about the primary client that may not be based on fact); (3) information that might be incorrectly used by other professionals who will see the client's records; and (4) information that could be subpoenaed and used in court against the client.

Gaining background information. In order to appropriately gain accurate background information concerning older clients, the practitioner and client will *define existing problems* and *examine solutions attempted.* Throughout the data gathering process, accurate probing provides necessary information concerning the client.

The service provider, interviewing older clients or referral sources in order to gain background information, will attempt to gain *specific* information concerning the reason for requesting services. Information about the problem that has caused the client to seek the provider's services will direct the questioning that follows. An adult daughter of an older woman may contact the director of a senior center requesting help in dealing with her mother. When questioned about the help she needs, the daughter may respond that her mother has lived in her home since having a stroke and that the current situation is "tense." What information does the director have about existing problems at this point? He knows that the elderly mother lives with her daughter and her family, that the mother has had a stroke and that the daughter is uncomfortable enough with the situation to seek the director's help. Beyond that, he knows very little. Prior to further questioning he must ask the daughter to provide her definition of tension, to describe who is affected by the tension, and to give *specific* examples of situations in which tension occurs in her home. The director's definition of "tense" may differ from the daughter's.

It is also helpful to request clients to discuss solutions that they have utilized in an attempt to solve their difficulties. Herr and Weakland (1979) suggest that the solutions older clients and their families have applied to problems may in fact have contributed to the problem situations. In addition, a family's attempts at solutions give the professional information about the way clients approach problems and also about their perception of this problem.

While asking questions to gain information about the client, *sensitive and appropriate* probing is necessary. Accurate probing of a client's situation to gather data involves sensitively seeking information that is honest and verifiable. Gambrill states,

> A typical assumption is that verbal reports accurately depict what happens in real-life settings. Since they may not, additional information should be gathered, for example by observation in the natural environment where this is feasible. Identification of the inferences you make and an insistence on substantiating these with strong rather than weak sources of evidence will allow you to offer more effective service since you will more readily identify and correct inaccurate judgments [1983: 4].

Brill (1985) suggests that the client's view (and verbal report) may not be accurate, but should be added as a part of the total summary of data gathered. This is important, as clients' perceptions of a situation are as real to them as are another individual's. Consequently, the information recorded in the final summary should *include, but qualify* that information that is reported by the client but that is questionable and not verifiable by other sources.

Accurate probing also involves checking out assumptions made from information provided. The following case example points to the importance of this.

Case Example 5.2

Mrs. Smith regularly visited her mother, Mrs. Ashton, at the long-term care facility where Mrs. Ashton was a resident. Because of a stroke, Mrs. Ashton was physically unable to feed herself. Mrs. Smith often came at mealtime and offered to feed her mother so that the nursing staff could "get on with more important work." After several weeks, Mrs. Smith complained to the head nurse that her mother refused to eat when she tried to feed her. She said that she encouraged her mother to eat and tried to help her in every way, but her mother would not cooperate.

The nurse, because of Mrs. Smith's regular visits and because of her own loving relationship with her mother, assumed that when Mrs. Smith encouraged Mrs. Ashton to eat, she did so in a supportive, caring manner. The nurse spoke with Mrs. Ashton about her refusal to be fed by her daughter, but Mrs. Ashton did not respond.

A week later, the nurse passed by Mrs. Ashton's room at mealtime and heard Mrs. Smith swear at her mother and tell her that if she did not eat, she would not visit her the following day.

Mrs. Smith and the nurse defined encouragement differently, although the nurse assumed that their definitions were similar.

Incorrect assumptions can be corrected in several ways. First, the service provider can ask older clients what they mean by certain words. For example: "Mrs. Smith, you mentioned that you encourage your mother to eat when you try to feed her. Can you tell me how you encourage her?" Requesting the client to detail specific behavior to which they refer is helpful. Second, the service provider can request the opportunity to observe older clients and their families interacting with one another. For example: "Mrs. Smith, you've told me that your mother gives you a difficult time when you try to feed her. I'd like to stop in during lunch today so that I can see some of her responses. I think that this might help me to better understand the problem." Third, the practitioner can contact other sources (requesting permission from the client when appropriate), who might provide clearer information about the situation. In the case above, the nurse might have noted that a nurse's aide often delivered and took Mrs. Ashton's food. The practitioner could have spoken with the aide in order to gain more insight into the problem.

Finally, appropriate probing can be enhanced by focusing on the total person and his or her situation. Approaching the client as *the problem* rather than as an individual *experiencing a problem* will prevent the client from having needs met. The practitioner who approaches each older client as an individual with strengths and weaknesses will be better able to gain information concerning the other systems with which the client is involved and the client's subsystems as well.

I recall a staff member in an outpatient mental health program referring to new clients as "another Mr. Green" or "another Mrs. Smith," implying that the new client had the same problems as did Mr. Green or Mrs. Smith. This staff member did not see older clients as the unique individuals that they were, but rather as a set of problems that she had to eradicate. Gambrill (1983) suggests the value of centering on the client's strengths rather than pathologies. Doing so allows the client to be viewed as a unique individual who has strengths that can be enhanced. Focusing on the client as the problem is only likely to label the client and increase the difficulties being experienced.

In the following case example, the service provider models the application of values, purpose, and knowledge to tasks during the data collection stage.

Case Example 5.3

Mrs. Chambers, a 78-year-old widow, was referred to the adult day care center by her daughter, Mrs. Sommers. After a brief initial interview with Mrs. Sommers and Mrs. Chambers, the intake worker, Miss Gibson, requested a meeting with Mrs. Chambers to gather necessary information. She suggested that the meeting be held in Mrs. Chambers' apartment. During the initial meeting, Miss Gibson obtained some background information about Mrs. Chambers, including income and ability to pay for the center's services.

MISS GIBSON: Mrs. Chambers, when we met last, I mentioned that I would need to have you provide me with some information about yourself. The information that you give me will help both of us to make a decision about whether or not you will come to the day care center. If we do decide that the center is something that would be useful to you and you want to come, the information you give will help us to plan a program for you that will be interesting to you.

MRS. CHAMBERS: What kind of information do you need?

MISS GIBSON: I will need to ask you about the activities you are involved in, the kinds of things you enjoy doing, your health, and your involvement with friends and family. If you do decide to come to the center, this information will help to determine the kinds of activities you would want to and would be able to join and to know the extent to which you would want your family to be involved. I want you to know that the information we discuss today will not be shared with anyone other than the staff at the day care center and I will only tell them the information that is necessary to help them know you and plan a program for you.

MRS. CHAMBERS: Will you tell anyone else what we talk about?

MISS GIBSON: Not unless I discuss it with you first and have your permission to do so. Mrs. Chambers, from talking to you last time, I have some information already. I have your full name as Mrs. Alice Chambers. When we visit the center next week, would you like to be introduced to the staff and center participants as Mrs. Chambers or as Alice?

MRS. CHAMBERS: Well, I hardly know them. I should think as Mrs. Chambers for now.

MISS GIBSON: That will be fine. Mrs. Chambers, last time we met, you and your daughter both told me that you are interested in the day care program because you would like to be around others during the day due to health problems. I wonder if you could tell me a little more about this.

MRS. CHAMBERS: I worry that something will happen during the day and that there will be no one here to help me. In the evening, my daughter comes over and visits for a while, but during the day no one is around.

MISS GIBSON: What might happen during the day that would require the help of others?

MRS. CHAMBERS: Well, I might fall and be unable to call for help.

MISS GIBSON: Have you fallen before?

MRS. CHAMBERS: Yes, several times. One time I had to wait on the bathroom floor for three hours before Cynthia (Mrs. Sommers) came for her evening visit.

MISS GIBSON: That must have been frightening.

MRS. CHAMBERS: Yes, it was very frightening. You can't imagine how afraid I was. I couldn't get up because of the pain and I worried that Cynthia would not come at all. Those three hours seemed to last for days.

MISS GIBSON: You mentioned pain. Were you hurt badly when you fell?

MRS. CHAMBERS: Yes. I broke my hip. I still need to use a walker as a result of that fall.

MISS GIBSON: How long ago did this happen?

MRS. CHAMBERS: Let me see. I guess it was a year and a half ago, because it was the week before my last birthday.

MISS GIBSON: Have you been living alone in your apartment since that time, with evening visits from your daughter?

MRS. CHAMBERS: Yes. I wish she could come during the day, too, but she works. I know its hard for her to come in the evening as it is, leaving her husband and children.

MISS GIBSON: Have you fallen since the time you broke your hip?

MRS. CHAMBERS: Only once and then I was able to get back up by myself.

MISS GIBSON: This must have been an extremely difficult time for you. Has there been anyone else who has been able to help?

MRS. CHAMBERS: Well, just the homemaker aide. She comes once a week to do some vacuuming. Other than that, there is only my son.

MISS GIBSON: Does your son live in town?

MRS. CHAMBERS: No, he lives 30 miles away. He and his family come in to see me every other week on Sundays. Right now they're planting crops and I remember how busy that keeps you. Dad and I used to work together every spring and I know how much time it takes to plant. They have no free time right now.

MISS GIBSON: Did you and your husband farm at one time?

MRS. CHAMBERS: All of our lives. Jack, our son, lives on the same farm now. He keeps things well tended to.

MISS GIBSON: When did you move from the farm?

MRS. CHAMBERS: Well, when Dad died, five years ago, Jack and his family moved in with me. Jack had been doing the work and it was easier for them to live there. After a year of living together, I knew it wouldn't work out. We're a close family, but Jack and his wife need privacy and so do I for that matter. We all agreed that it would be best for me to live in the city near Cynthia.

MISS GIBSON: That must have been quite a change after so many years. Was it difficult to move?

MRS. CHAMBERS: Certainly. But I'd do it again. I won't live with either of my children. I'd rather live apart than together and have resentment on both sides. That could have happened if I'd stayed with Jack.

MISS GIBSON: Getting along well with your children is very important to you.

MRS. CHAMBERS: Yes, it is. We were always a close family and have enjoyed being together a good deal. I think children and grand-children are the greatest joy a person can have.

MISS GIBSON: What kinds of things do you and your family do together, now that the children are grown?

MRS. CHAMBERS: Oh, we celebrate holidays together. We still all go out to the farm. Either Cynthia or Jack take me to a concert occasionally and the grandchildren often stop by to see me. I only wish that I wasn't so dependent. It would be nice to still be back on the farm and to be able to take care of myself, but I know I wouldn't be happy there now. That's why I wanted to move.

MISS GIBSON: It sounds as though you wanted to move, but that living alone has its difficulties as well. You have tried several things to make that easier, though. Have you tried anything other than the home-maker aide or having Cynthia stop by nightly?

MRS. CHAMBERS: Well, not really. I call Cynthia at work every morning and afternoon. If she doesn't hear from me, she knows to check up on me. I worry, that I bother her there. I know that going to the day care center would put my mind at ease during the day and would also lighten Cynthia's load.

MISS GIBSON: I find myself wondering how you get along at night after Cynthia is gone. Are you concerned about being alone then?

MRS. CHAMBERS: No. Cynthia comes just before my bedtime. She stays until I'm in bed at 10:00.

MISS GIBSON: Do you sleep well during the night?

MRS. CHAMBERS: Yes, I still sleep soundly until it gets light outside.

MISS GIBSON: Do you have neighbors or friends or other relatives who stop by occasionally?

MRS. CHAMBERS: I have no living relatives besides my children and grandchildren. My sister died 15 years ago after a long illness. We were never very close. She was my only other living relative. Most of my friends lived in the small town near our farm. I've been able to make a few friends here. The van from the senior center picks me up once a week and I go to lunch there. I enjoy the people I've met there, but I only talk to them on the telephone occasionally. We don't visit in each other's homes, because it's hard to get around, you know.

MISS GIBSON: Is it difficult to get transportation to the places you would like to go?

MRS. CHAMBERS: My daughter and her husband will take me anywhere I want to go, but during the day, I'm unable to get around except when the van takes me to the senior center.

MISS GIBSON: Where would you go if you had a car and could drive?

MRS. CHAMBERS: I suppose I'd go visit some of the women I've met during the noon meals at the senior center. I've come to know several of them well and have even been invited to their homes. It would be nice to see friends often.

MISS GIBSON: Do you have any neighbors whom you see regularly?

MRS. CHAMBERS: Yes, I see Mrs. O'Neil, across the hall. She stops by to gossip and have tea most afternoons.

MISS GIBSON: Do you enjoy her visits?

MRS. CHAMBERS: Oh my, yes. She's quite a character you know. Always knows what's going on in the building. We're both widows, too, so we have that in common. We enjoy each other's company and make each other less lonely.

MISS GIBSON: You mentioned earlier that you are a widow and that your husband had died five years ago.

MRS. CHAMBERS: Yes.

MISS GIBSON: You were both still on the farm when he died?

MRS. CHAMBERS: Yes we were. I didn't expect him to die so soon. He was only 73. I had hoped that we would have more good years together.

MISS GIBSON: Your years together were good.

MRS. CHAMBERS: Yes, they were. Oh, we had our ups and downs, but worked hard together and cared for each other a great deal.

MISS GIBSON: Was your husband ill before his death?

MRS. CHAMBERS: No, he wasn't. His death was totally unexpected.

MISS GIBSON: That must have been a very hard time for you.

MRS. CHAMBERS: Yes. It's still hard, although it does get easier as time goes on. I suppose it's something you never get over.

MISS GIBSON: Can you tell me the things that have helped make it easier?

MRS. CHAMBERS: Well, my children help by remembering the happy times we all had with Dad and by being with me when I've been especially sad. They come by on our anniversaries and we talk about Dad. It helps me to talk about it with my family. Mrs. O'Neil and I talk too. We're two old women who have both lost our husbands.

MISS GIBSON: It does help to be able to talk to someone who has had a similar experience. I'm glad to hear that your family is willing to talk about your husband with you and that you can share your feelings, both happy and sad, with them. How many years were you and your husband married?

MRS. CHAMBERS: We were sweethearts in school. When Dad quit school after the eighth grade to help his father on the farm, we courted until I was 18. We married on my eighteenth birthday. We were married 55 years.

MISS GIBSON: That's a long time.

MRS. CHAMBERS: Yes, yes it was. A good time as well. I'm glad I have my children and grandchildren.

MISS GIBSON: Tell me about your children's families.

MRS. CHAMBERS: Well Cynthia and her husband have three boys. They are all teenagers now. Nice boys. They come to see me sometimes and the two oldest, David and John can drive. They take me to the grocery store when Cynthia is busy. Cynthia's husband is a good fellow, but he's no farmer! He's a city boy, but he makes a good husband to Cynthia and he's a good son-in-law. Jack and his wife have two daughters. Isn't that ironic! Cynthia who lives in the city has sons and Jack who needs boys to help has daughters! His girls are in college now. They are good students and have a lot of boyfriends. Yes, I have a good family. Do you know those girls write to me from college, as busy as they are! I send them cookies every so often. I know they get homesick for home-cooked food. They always come to see me on vacation and their mother has me out to the farm for dinner whenever they are back from school.

MISS GIBSON: It sounds as though your family enjoys you as much as you enjoy them.

MRS. CHAMBERS: Yes, I believe that they do.

MISS GIBSON: Mrs. Chambers, we talked about your health a little earlier. I'd like to ask a few more questions. Do you take any medication?

MRS. CHAMBERS: No, I don't. Not since my hip quit hurting. That's good for a 78-year-old woman, isn't it?

MISS GIBSON: It certainly is. Do you have any physical problems other than your hip?

MRS. CHAMBERS: No. I'm grateful for that. Oh, I can't see as well as I used to and my hip slows me down, but I'm healthy.

MISS GIBSON: You certainly look healthy. Do you remember when you had your last physical examination?

MRS. CHAMBERS: That would be two months ago. They had me in to look at my hip and gave me a complete check up. The doctor said that I was in good shape, but that I should still use the walker.

MISS GIBSON: You mentioned that you eat lunch at the senior center once a week. Do you cook for yourself the rest of the time?

MRS. CHAMBERS: Yes, I enjoy cooking, although it's not the same cooking for one person. I usually make a roast or a ham once a week and then I have enough left over for several meals. I only cook at night. I eat a sandwich for lunch and cereal in the morning.

MISS GIBSON: If you should come to the day care center, are there any activities you would be interested in doing there?

MRS. CHAMBERS: Well, I noticed women quilting when Cynthia and I stopped by the other day. I would certainly like that. I've quilted for years. I also like music. The children take me to concerts and I play the piano myself. Do you have any music activities?

MISS GIBSON: Yes we do. In fact, several of the participants get together and play instruments occasionally. We have a piano, but no pianist. They could certainly use someone who could play the piano!

MRS. CHAMBERS: Well, I just may be their person.

MISS GIBSON: Mrs. Chambers, you have been very helpful. You've given me information that will help us when we meet at the center next week to have you look our program over and to discuss whether you would like to be a part of our program. It would help me if I could talk to your physician about the activities that would be suitable for you. Could I have your permission to ask your physician for information about you?

MRS. CHAMBERS: Yes, if that would help.

MISS GIBSON: I think it would. I also wondered if you would be willing to let me talk to your daughter about her feelings concerning the day care center. Could I call her and speak with her?

MRS. CHAMBERS: Certainly.

MISS GIBSON: In that case, I'll call both your physician and your daughter before we meet on Wednesday. I will plan to see you and your daughter at the day care center next Wednesday afternoon. Thank you so much for your time. You were very helpful.

Miss Gibson carried out the tasks of showing her client *respect, increasing Mrs. Chambers comfort,* and *gaining appropriate information in a sensitive manner.* She did this in several ways.

Miss Gibson showed her client *respect* throughout the interview. She established this by clearly explaining her reasons for needing information and to what use the information would be put. She let Mrs. Chambers know that the information she provided would be used when they made a decision about whether Mrs. Chambers would participate in the program. If Mrs. Chambers decided to do so, the information would help the staff plan an appropriate program for her.

In order to make Mrs. Chambers more *comfortable,* Mrs. Gibson scheduled the meeting in Mrs. Chambers' apartment. This functioned to ensure confidentiality during the interview. Mrs. Chambers was aware that, in this setting, others could not listen to her responses to Miss Gibson's questions.

In addition, by meeting on Mrs. Chambers' "territory," Miss Gibson gave her client some control over this stage of the relationship. Mrs. Chambers did not have to come into a foreign setting and provide information concerning herself. Rather, she was in an environment that, because of its familiarity, provided a sense of safety for her. Because of this, Mrs. Chambers did not need to spend the interview adjusting to a new setting as well as a new intake worker. Rather, she was in a setting that provided support and thus enhanced her ability to adjust to Miss Gibson. In social systems terminology, Mrs. Chambers' sense of comfort in her apartment provided her with the energy to relate to Miss Gibson in a more functional manner. Consequently, Mrs. Chambers' need to cope was met through the setting.

Finally, comfort was established through Miss Gibson's statements that Mrs. Chambers had a choice as to whether or not to come to the day care center. Some older individuals are made to feel, by their families and by service providers, that they have no choice as to whom their caregivers will be. Clearly stating that the client does have a choice enhances his or her sense of control over the situation and provides the client with the impetus to make appropriate choices.

Miss Gibson *gathered accurate information in a sensitive way* by using several skills. First, she did not read a list of questions to her client. Instead, she allowed Mrs. Chambers to talk, to review parts of her life while asking questions related to the subjects being discussed. When the interview was over, the areas listed on the Data Gathering Format were answered, but were provided by Mrs. Chambers in a sequence that was meaningful to her. Consequently, Miss Gibson not only has the basic information she requires, but also has a perception of how Mrs. Chambers perceives her life and her current situation. This is necessary to making an assessment and setting service priorities.

When Mrs. Chambers strayed from the topic, Miss Gibson would gently bring her back by restating a question. When a question was not answered, Miss Gibson asked it again. For example, she first asked, "Do you have neighbors or friends or other relatives who stop by occasionally?" Mrs. Chambers answered that question partially and they discussed another topic. Later, Miss Gibson asked, "Do you have any neighbors whom you see regularly?"

Summarizing was used to keep the discussion on target and to lead to new areas of information. For example, Miss Gibson stated, "It sounds as though you wanted to move, but that living alone has its difficulties as well." She then brought the conversation around to the types of support that Mrs. Chambers had utilized.

Miss Gibson applied the values, purpose, and knowledge of the information gathering stage to the tasks she utilized when inter-

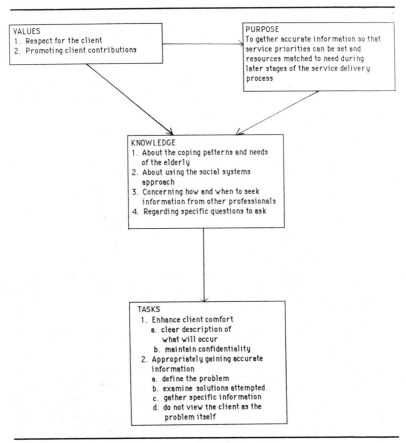

Figure 5.1: Service Provision Framework: Gathering Data

viewing Mrs. Chambers. By doing so, she gained necessary information, furthered the trust between her client and herself, and allowed Mrs. Chambers to meet the basic needs of coping, expressing herself, contributing to her own welfare, and gaining some control. Mrs. Chambers, as a social system, has exchanged information with Miss Gibson and received external support from her. Mrs. Chambers relationship with Miss Gibson will contribute to her adjustment to the day care center if she does decide to participate in that program.

CONCLUSION

The data gathering phase of the service delivery process involves adhering to the values of respecting the client and promoting the client's contributions to the service delivery process. These values influence the purpose of this phase, which is to gather information for setting service priorities and matching resources to needs during later phases of the client-professional relationship. The knowledge needed to appropriately gather data includes knowledge about the elderly, use of the social systems approach, gaining information from other professionals, and specific questions to ask. Values, purpose, and knowledge direct the tasks of enhancing client comfort with the questioning and appropriately gaining accurate information. This is depicted in Figure 5.1.

The human service worker can gather data from clients and relevant others in a manner that forges linkages and allows for energy exchanges with clients. Throughout this phase of the service delivery process, basic needs of the client can be met.

In the following chapter, assessment and setting service priorities will be discussed. Case 5.3 will be assessed from a social systems perspective and priorities will be set for matching resources to the needs experienced by Mrs. Chambers.

APPENDIX
Data Gathering Format

BACKGROUND INFORMATION ON CLIENT

Client's full name _____

Name client prefers to be called (Mrs. _____ , first name or
    nickname) _____

Client's description of the problem that brought about your agency's involvement
    (specific aspects of the problem, duration of the problem, factors surrounding the
    problem) _____
    _____
    _____

Client's address _____

    How long has client lived at that address? _____

    Previous address if client has moved within last year _____
    _____

    Does the client live alone? _____ If not, with whom does the client live and what is
    their relationship to the client? _____

Client's telephone number _____

Client's birthday _____

Client's birthplace _____

    If client was not born in the United States, what is the client's primary language?
    _____

Client's ethnic and cultural background _____
    _____
    _____
    _____

What is the client's educational level? _____

Is the client employed? _____ If yes, what is the name of the client's employer?
    _____

    What is the client's position? _____

    If not, is the client retired? _____ If yes, what was the nature of the client's
    employment prior to retirement? _____
    _____

What is the client's socioeconomic status? _____

    What are the sources of the client's income? _____
    _____

    Does the client qualify for any income that he or she is not currently receiving?
    _____
    _____

    Is the client's income sufficient? _____

What is the client's housing situation? (Does the client own or rent? Is the client's
    home in a safe neighborhood? Does the home have adequate space, heating, and
    ventilization?) _____

APPENDIX Continued

How are the client's transportation needs met? (Does the client have a car? Is he or she able to drive? When he or she needs to shop, who takes him or her?)

_____

Client's physician:
name _____
address _____
telephone number _____
Brief description of client's physical appearance _____

Does the client currently, or has the client in the past received services from any formal agencies? _____ If so, list the agencies, describe what services were provided, when they were provided, and the duration of the client's involvement with the agencies _____

_____

What are the client's feelings concerning the services received? (Were expectations met? Why or why not? Did the client find the services helpful? Why or why not?)

_____

CLIENT'S FAMILY BACKGROUND

Marital status:
Single? _____ If so, has the client been divorced? When did the divorce occur? _____ What are the client's feelings concerning the divorce?

_____

Widowed? _____ If so, what was the length of the marriage? _____
When did the spouse die?
Client's response to and current feelings concerning spouse's death (Has client grieved for spouse? What is the client's affect when discussing spouse?) _____

_____

_____

Was this the client's first marriage? _____ If not, what ended previous marriages?

_____

What impact have earlier marriages had on the client? _____

_____

Married? _____ If yes, what is spouse's name and age?

_____

Does spouse reside with the client? _____
What is the length of current marriage? _____

(continued)

Ask client to describe his or her relationship to current partner (What aspects of the relationship are or are not satisfactory to the client? Is one partner dominant in the relationship? How are tasks divided between partners? If there are children, how does each partner relate to them?) _____

_____

_____

_____

_____

Children:

Does the client have children? _____ If so, what is the name, age, address, and telephone number of each child: _____

_____

_____

_____

Describe the client's relationship to his or her children (Which aspects of the relationship are satisfactory to the client and which are not? How often does the client see his or her children? How often do they talk on the telephone? Do the client's children provide any type of support to the client, such as helping around the home, shopping, financial support, etc.? If so, what are the client's feelings about the support received? Does the client provide any support to his or her children? If so, what does that involve? What are the client's feelings about the support he or she provides?) _____

_____

_____

Have any of the client's children died? _____ If so, how recently? _____

Names and ages of children at the time of death _____

Discuss with client his or her response to the child's death _____

_____

_____

Grandchildren:

Does the client have grandchildren? _____ If so, list their names, ages, and addresses _____

How frequently does the client see or talk to grandchildren? _____

Describe the client's relationship with his or her grandchildren (include aspects outlined under relationship with children) _____

_____

APPENDIX Continued

Siblings:
Does the client have any living siblings? _____ If so, list their names, ages and addresses? _____

How frequently does the client see or talk to siblings? _____

Describe the client's relationship with his or her siblings (include aspects outlined under relationships with children) _____

Have any of the client's siblings died? _____ If so, how recently? _____
What were the circumstances of their deaths? _____

What is the client's response to the death of siblings? _____

Are there any other family members with whom client is involved (nieces, nephews, cousins, in-laws, etc.)? _____ If so, what are their names and addresses?
_____

How frequently do they see or talk to the client? _____
_____ What is the nature of their relationship with the client? _____
_____

SOCIAL BACKGROUND

Friends and neighbors:
Does the client have any close friends or neighbors? _____ If yes, what are their names, addresses, and telephone numbers? _____
_____

What is the nature of their relationship? (Include aspects outlined under relationship with children) _____

Have any close friends or neighbors moved away or died recently? _____ If yes, discuss clients feelings concerning this _____
_____

Memberships:
Is the client a member of any formal or informal groups? _____ If yes, list and discuss client's participation _____
_____

CLIENT'S PSYCHOLOGICAL STATUS

Is the client oriented to person, place, and time? _____
Describe the client's ability to remember recent and past events _____
_____

(continued)

If the client has been given any intelligence tests, list the test and the results

_____
Who administered the test? _____
Does the client exhibit any signs of depression? (Pessimism about the future? Feelings of uselessness? Crying spells? Unusually fearful? Irritability? Loneliness? Hypochondriacal symptoms? Sleep difficulties? Weight loss? Bowel impaction?) _____
If so, discuss the symptoms and their onset _____

_____

Discuss the client's life experiences with the client. Does the client express feelings of acceptance, satisfaction, dissatisfaction or guilt concerning the way he or she has lived life? _____

Has the client ever received formal treatment for emotional problems? _____ If yes, discuss _____

_____

CLIENT'S PHYSICAL STATUS

How does the client describe his or her physical situation? _____

_____
When did the client last have a complete physical exam? _____
What were the results of the examination? _____
Is the client suffering from any chronic or acute physical ailments? _____
Is the client currently taking any medication? _____ If yes, list the medications taken

_____
Is the client mobile? _____
Is the client continent? _____
Can the client bathe him or herself? _____
Can the client carry out tasks and activities that he or she desires? _____ If not, what physical factors prohibit this? _____

_____
How many hours does the client sleep nightly? _____ What time does the client go to bed and arise? _____
Does the client take naps? _____
Has the client had any problem with falling? _____ If yes, describe the frequency with which this occurs _____
Describe the meals eaten by the client in a typical day _____

_____
Are there sexual issues of concern to the client? _____

_____

OTHER

Does religion play an important role in the client's life? _____ If so, what is the

APPENDIX Continued

client's religious affiliation? _____

and in what way is religion meaningful to the client? _____

_____

Does the client have any hobbies or interests that have not been discussed?

_____

Would the client (or other resource person) wish to add any information to that which has already been provided? _____

_____

_____

Is there another person with whom the client would like the service provider to talk?

_____

6

ESTABLISHING SERVICE PRIORITIES

The human service worker enters this stage of service provision with information about the older client system and other relevant social systems. In order to meet the client's needs successfully, goals for service delivery are established. *Both assessment and setting goals are components of establishing service priorities.* Through assessment, vital knowledge about clients' needs is provided. *Setting goals* helps to ensure that the intervention with the client will be purposeful and will meet the client's needs. Within this chapter, priority setting and related aspects will be described. Following this, discussion will center on the values, purpose, knowledge, and skills required for successful service delivery at this stage.

SETTING SERVICE PRIORITIES

Assessment. Assessment is an important part of the priority setting process as it provides both the human service worker and the elderly client with information that will determine goals to be set. What is involved in assessing the material obtained in the data gathering stage? Certainly some assessment takes place during the process of gaining information about the client. Assessment during the data gathering stage directs the questioning of the service provider. After the service provider has talked with the client and relevant others, the data will be put into meaningful order. As Epstein (1980: 13) states, "Assessment consists of *finding out* the problems (exploration), together with *classification* and *specification* of the problems. The influential conditions in the environment, *the problem context,* should be identified."

In addition to examining problems that the elderly client is experiencing, assessment functions to provide the practitioner with a picture of the total client. Although a number of clients may experience similar problems, the manner in which these problems should be met will differ because of the individual characteristics and situation of each older client. Consequently, the service provider who utilizes a social systems perspective in assessing the client's situation will be aware of the varied and individual strengths and needs of each client and will be best prepared to work with the client to set goals to meet needs and utilize strengths. As will be discussed below, assessment is not the individual task of the service provider, but takes place in concert with the client.

Setting goals. Setting goals involves applying knowledge gained from assessment in order to plan *with the client* what services will be provided. This stage of the service delivery process includes establishing what the client wishes to accomplish, making a joint determination as to whether the client's goals are appropriate as well as delegating the work and resources necessary to achieve the client's goals.

Working with elderly clients to set service priorities, the service provider will act on *values,* carry out a *purpose,* apply *knowledge,* and utilize *skills.* Throughout this process, the service provider benefits from an awareness of basic needs and from maintaining a social systems perspective.

Values

The basic values of service provision are reflected in the values called on at this stage of the service delivery process. These values include (1) the belief that *elderly clients' needs are important;* (2) the recognition that *older clients have the right to be self-determining;* (3) the acknowledgement that *clients should not be provided with unrealistic expectations;* and (4) the belief that the *clients' needs should be met in a manner that does not prevent others from meeting their needs.*

Importance of clients' needs. Elderly clients and/or their families may come to the service provider having clearly defined their needs for themselves. A basic value at this stage is to set priorities that will match resources to the needs perceived and experienced by the client. In attempting to ensure that older clients have access to resources that will allow them to meet their needs and reach their potentials, it is important to attend to the needs expressed by clients. If a client or family member's stated wishes are inappropriate, the human service worker has the responsibility to inform them that this is the case. However, when this occurs, the practitioner and older client benefit from a joint determination as to how the client's desires can realistically be adjusted so that appropriate resources can be provided.

As Case Example 6.1 indicates, the assessment and goal setting process is most successfully accomplished when an intervention schedule is established that is directed toward appropriately meeting the needs felt by the older client.

Case Example 6.1

Mr. Jacobs is a social worker employed by the county Department of Human Services. He has met with his 75-year-old client, Miss Winley, on several occasions. Having gathered background information concerning her needs, Mr. Jacobs and Miss Winley are currently in the process of assessing her situation and establishing service delivery goals.

Miss Winley was referred to Mr. Jacobs because she recently had a stroke and was partially paralyzed. Miss Winley's niece, who lived in a distant city, had called Mr. Jacobs' agency and expressed concern about her aunt living alone. Mr. Jacobs had met with Miss Winley, spoken with the niece over the telephone, and talked with several of Miss Winley's neighbors who had been providing some help to her.

Mr. Jacobs established a trusting relationship with Miss Winley and she expressed to him her anger about having a stroke and being unable to care for herself as she wished to do. When the two met to review the information that had been gathered and to establish service priorities, Miss Winley stated that she believed she could continue to live on her own and would like to do so without receiving services from formal agencies. She said the help provided by her neighbors was adequate and she would like to continue with this. Mr. Jacobs felt that this was inappropriate for several reasons. First, the neighbors had indicated to him that they could not continue to help Miss Winley indefinitely as they had other obligations. Second, even if the neighbors had been willing to continue helping Miss Winley, the help they were providing was insufficient. Miss Winley was only eating one meal a day. She had developed bed sores and her personal hygiene was inadequate for her health.

Mr. Jacobs shared with Miss Winley the concerns of her neighbors and expressed his own concern about nutrition and hygiene. They then reassessed her situation together, based on the information that had been gathered in the previous phase, and attempted to establish service priorities that could most closely meet with Miss Winley's desires while at the same time realistically provide for the actual needs she was experiencing.

In Case Example 6.1, Mr. Jacobs believed that his client's perceived needs were important. However, he also recognized that her suggestions for meeting these needs were not appropriate, as they could not be met in the way she desired. Because he responded to her stated need and then helped her modify that so that appropriate goals could be set, the client was able to feel valued. Consequently, her trust in the worker was strengthened and she allowed him to facilitate her attempt to meet coping needs. Finally, she was made a part of this stage of the service delivery process.

In addition to attending to the client's expressed needs, it is possible for the service provider to assume that the older client has needs beyond those expressed. For example, an elderly couple may approach a service provider with a concern about their living situation. In the course of gathering background information, the service provider may determine that the couple has had difficulty in relating to one of their adult children. The service provider could establish an agenda that would attempt to work out the problems between parents and child. This is appropriate *if* the practitioner has asked the older couple if they would like to work on this issue and the couple has agreed that they would like to improve their relationship with their child. If this has not occurred, the goal of working toward bettering the parent-child relationship may meet the service provider's need to enhance relationships, but not necessarily the elderly couple's needs.

Assessment and setting goals for service should not extend beyond the areas of the client's expressed concern unless it is necessary to do so in order to meet the client's stated need. The value of attending to the client's expressed needs dictates that the service provider's task at this stage is to deal with the problem at hand, first through assessment and then through setting goals. Assessment is different from diagnosis. When assessing, "observable behaviors are not used as signs of something more significant but as important in their own right as *samples* of relevant behaviors. Behavior is considered to be a response to identifiable environmental or personal events such as specific thoughts or feelings" (Gambrill, 1983: 34). With every older client, as with all individuals, assessment may reveal numerous areas that could benefit from change. The service provider who extends "help" beyond what the client desires is not establishing the client's needs as primary.

The client's right to self-determination. The value of elderly client self-determination has been discussed in relation to earlier phases of service delivery. When establishing service priorities, client self-determination indicates that clients will be expected to join with the service provider in evaluating their situations and in setting goals to deal with the problems they are experiencing. The value of client self-determination would suggest that the elderly client and service provider work together in assessing the client's situation and setting goals.

The process of joining with the client to assess and set goals has several advantages. Partnership in this process protects the client's individuality and maximizes opportunities for exercise of self-determination. In discussions, negotiations, and choosing among available alternatives, or in making commitments to engage in developing new alternatives, the client's opportunities for meaningful decisions about self and situation are greatly increased [Compton and Galaway, 1984: 396].

Service providers who doubt the client's right to become involved in this stage of the process "may partially account for the limited involvement of some clients in the helping process or their withdrawal from it" (Maluccio and Marlow, 1984: 412). Likewise, as Berger and Anderson (1984: 456) suggest, workers who view the elderly client as unable to become involved because of physical or other incapacities, "may thereby undermine the clients' potential for self-care and independence."

Obviously, some frail older clients are unable to join fully in the service delivery process. For these individuals, service delivery is enhanced by encouraging their involvement to the greatest possible extent, along with the involvement of family or friends who care about them. Expecting older clients' participation at this stage will serve to facilitate their self-determination. Denying their right to involvement will give the message that they are helpless or unworthy of making decisions concerning their lives, while providing for self-determination facilitates older clients in having influence over their lives.

Providing realistic information about expected results. Service providers facilitate the process of setting goals when they strive to be honest and open with older clients about what they can expect from the services that will be provided. When setting goals with aged clients, it is particularly important *not* to establish goals that are beyond the client's ability to accomplish or that call for more extensive resources than exist. Setting unrealistic goals results in giving older clients false hope. False hope, of course, can either result in betraying the trust older clients have placed in the worker or in leading clients to become even more discouraged about their situations and the possibility of meeting their needs.

Clients' needs and the needs of others. The needs of others related to the older client are also valued by the human service worker. It is hoped that the data gathering process will have provided information about other individuals involved with the older client. This information should be utilized in assessment and in setting goals for service provision. As social systems, older clients respond to needs by adapting and then adapt again when their needs are met. This invariably has an influence on the functioning of others around them. If the adaptations of aged clients conflict with the need meeting of others to whom they are linked, the client will then have to expend energy to deal with ensuing problems.

In addition to forestalling future problems for the older client by considering the needs of others, the service provider is also modeling how clients can act responsibly toward others. The belief that older clients have a responsibility to others in society can be employed at this stage, when clients are determining how they will deal with their problems. The message to elderly clients is that when problems occur, they are not alone in dealing with them *or* in being affected by them. In addition, this sets the stage for meeting the contributory needs of the aged client.

Purpose

As the client and service provider meet to develop service priorities, their purpose is twofold. First, *provider and client strive to assess information and to set goals.* In attempting to match resources to need, assessment must be thorough and goals should be developed that, when carried out, will enable the client to function more successfully. Consequently, the goals set will be related to the needs that have been established through an assessment of the information that has been gathered. The result should be a plan to forge linkages with social systems that can provide energy to enhance the client's ability to maintain balance.

A second purpose is *to facilitate clients in learning the process of assessing needs and appropriately setting goals for problems that they encounter.* It is expected that service provision will increase the elderly client's ability to cope as independently as possible. As assessment is accomplished and goals are set, the service provider is teaching the older client (as well as others involved in the service delivery process) the steps involved in working on problems that occur. In the future, clients can apply this knowledge and feel more competent in dealing with the difficulties that they encounter. They will know more about how to evaluate their situations and where to look for resources that can meet their needs.

Knowledge

The service provider requires knowledge relative to assessing older client's situations and setting goals with older clients. Knowledge in this area encompasses: (1) a *knowledge of which factors are relevant* to the problem at hand and *which factors are not involved;* (2) an *awareness that older clients are knowledgeable* about their situations and needs; and (3) a *knowledge of resources available* to match the needs of the client.

Knowledge of factors relevant to the problem. The practitioner requires background knowledge that will facilitate recognition of relevant aspects of the client's problem. Some of this knowledge will be gained through *formal training* and some through *experiences* with other older clients. *Formal training* provides information about the elderly population. It will inform the worker of the fact that the aged are individuals and that they experience situations differently, based on their backgrounds, their own personal characteristics, and the social systems with which they are involved. Formal education will also provide the practitioner with knowledge about utilizing a social systems approach in analyzing a client's situation.

Experience also gives the practitioner background knowledge from which to draw. Experience presents information concerning the following: aspects of assessment that have been accurate and inaccurate in the past with other older clients; the types of goals that have been appropriate and inappropriate in other similar situations; and the kinds of work that are most suited to certain types of problems and client characteristics.

It is valuable to recognize, however, that knowledge about the elderly population and experiences with older clients are alone insufficient to assess and set goals for service delivery. It may be that training and experience will lead the provider to place importance on things that would have been suitable in other situations with other clients, but not appropriate in the current situation with this client. As a result, service providers will want to *combine the knowledge they have with information about the specific older client with whom they are working.*

Awareness of the older client's knowledge. As noted, the service provider is not alone in possessing knowledge concerning the client's problem and the client's ability to meet goals. Elderly clients and their families often know their own strengths and can provide helpful information about how those strengths can be used to resolve a difficulty they are experiencing. The service provider brings knowledge from training and experience. However, the elderly client brings knowledge that the provider does not have prior to the development of their relationship. This includes knowledge of his or her own strengths and weaknesses, knowledge about what types of solutions would be viewed as satisfactory, and knowledge about what has and has not worked in solving problems in the past. Involved family members, too, bring information central to assessment and goal setting.

Compton and Galaway (1983: 397) stress that the process of combining the provider's and client's knowledge is of value. "This process involves the ordering and organizing of the information, intuitions, and knowledge that client and worker bring so that the pieces come together into some pattern that makes sense . . . in explaining the problem and in relating the explanation to alternative solutions." Awareness *and use* of the older client's knowledge can lead to a more thorough and accurate assessment of the client's situation and can help target goals more appropriately. Requesting information from older clients and/or family members at this stage affords the opportunity for sharing their previous attempts at assessment and goal setting. Getzel (1983) discusses group work with caregiving family and friends of the elderly. He states that these individuals have already attempted solutions to their problems. Sharing these clearly allows them to identify their own strengths and weaknesses.

Knowledge of available resources. In setting goals with older clients, it is necessary to be aware of the resources that are available to meet the client's needs. Lack of information about services that exist can artificially narrow the solutions available to the older client. Elderly clients are denied the ability to cope to their fullest potential when practitioners do not educate themselves as to the availability of resources for their clients.

Awareness of services must be supplemented by a determination of their availability. It is likely that a variety of resources exist that can potentially aid the client. However, following assessment and prior to establishing goals, it is important to verify that the desired resources are available. For example, an older client wishing to remain in her own home may be gratified to learn from the service provider that a homemaker aide can come to help her several times a week. If the provider has not determined the availability of the homemaker aide prior to "promising" the services, the client may be disappointed to find herself on a long waiting list. In addition to being denied immediately needed services, the client may feel that her situation is more hopeless than before and may possibly lose confidence in the worker.

Knowledge about assessment and setting goals is enhanced by tasks that are enacted at this stage. Through skillful application of values, purpose, and knowledge, the service provider can better establish appropriate service priorities.

Tasks

The human service worker providing direct services to elderly clients has a series of tasks that must be undertaken in order to establish service priorities. First, the worker requires skill in *involving the client in the assessment and goal setting process.* Second, the service provider will want to engage in the task of *determining the older client's weakness and strengths and the appropriate resources relevant to those.* The third task involves *ensuring that the goals that are set are attainable.* Fourth, the service provider has the task of *developing a contract with the older client and other formal and informal service providers.* Throughout the process of developing service priorities, the worker strives to educate older clients so that they can apply what they have learned to future situations they encounter.

Involving the client. The value of involving the client and/or significant others in setting service priorities has been discussed above. Some elderly clients will wish to participate in setting priorities and will either instigate their involvement or will join in when requested. Others, however, will be less willing to engage in this task.

If trust between practitioner and aged client system has not been established or maintained, the client and significant others are likely to withdraw at this point. When this occurs, clients and other involved support systems may feel that the service worker is attempting to violate boundaries that have been carefully guarded. If this is the case, the worker must retrace the steps taken and attempt to establish trust with the older client system, calling on skills discussed in earlier chapters.

It may be that elderly clients or family members have come to the service provider for assistance hoping that an individual other than themselves would be asked to work toward change. When they realize that they will be expected to be involved in the change process, they may resist. If members of the client system do not wish to take responsibility for change, the service provider has the task of redetermining their desire for change to occur. An open discussion asking the client and involved others to recall reasons for wishing to become involved with the service provider is helpful, as is a reminder that if they wish change, they must take responsibility to bring about change. The extent of confrontation should depend on both the members of the client system and the relationship that has been established. The personality of the individual client family member is an important consideration. For some individuals, strong confrontation will cause them to try to save face by further entrenching themselves in their stated position. In contrast, other older clients may only respond to strong confrontation. In addition, an unstable worker-client relationship may be less able to withstand confrontation than a firmly established one. An awareness of both the aged client's personality and the status of the relationship will guide the provider concerning the approaches to be taken in this situation.

Clients or family members also may resist involvement at this stage of the process if the balance they have effected is too tenuous, causing the idea of change to be frightening. Case Example 6.2 illustrates this. When the client chooses not to become involved due to fear of change, the provider can attempt to become a source of energy that will aid the older person in making necessary adaptations and, consequently, in meeting coping needs.

Case Example 6.2

Mrs. Janke is a 72-year-old widow who resides with her son, his wife, and their teenage daughter. Mrs. Conley, an outreach worker for the community mental health center, was asked by Mrs. Janke's niece to visit Mrs. Janke. The niece had indicated that she felt Mrs. Janke was unhappy in her current situation and requested that Mrs. Conley meet with her to determine her feelings. Mrs. Conley has met with Mrs. Janke in the Janke home on three occasions. Mrs. Janke has stated that she would like to establish regular meetings with Mrs. Conley to talk about how she could improve her living situation. She related that she and her daughter-in-law have arguments about numerous issues.

Mrs. Janke has lived with her son and his family for one year. The move to her son's home was overwhelming to her, as she did not want to leave her own home; but she and her son both felt that because of her physical condition, she should not live alone. Mrs. Janke felt strongly that she did not want to enter a nursing home and finally agreed to move in with her son.

At the time of each of their meetings, Mrs. Conley has noticed that Mrs. Janke has had cuts on her face and bruises in different stages of healing. Once Mrs. Janke's scalp was bleeding as though her hair as been pulled. Mrs. Janke was actively involved in the process of assessing her situation until Mrs. Conley questioned her about her injuries. After revealing that she was being physically abused by her daughter-in-law, Mrs. Janke appeared to lose interest in the relationship. She stated that things between her daughter-in-law and herself had improved. She said that she would like to continue to see Mrs. Conley but that she primarily wanted their relationship to be a friendship.

It may be that Mrs. Janke is choosing not to become involved in planning for change due to a fear of the adjustments that change will require. She could be concerned that change will include moving to a long-term care facility or that planning for change will bring about more abuse from her daughter-in-law. Mrs. Janke has already made adaptations in order to live in her current situation. Further adjustments may seem impossible to her. It would be helpful for Mrs. Conley to provide external energy to her client by letting her know that she will stay involved and support her as well as by offering to meet with both Mrs. Janke and family members to work on the problems they are experiencing. If the family wants Mrs. Janke to stay in the home and they are willing to work to bring about change, Mrs. Conley can offer this information to Mrs. Janke. Mrs. Conley would also need to report the abuse of her client to the appropriate organization. Prior to doing this, she can involve her client by sharing that she is mandated ethically and legally (if this is the case) to report abuse. Mrs. Conley will also want to tell Mrs. Janke's family that she is required to report the abuse, if giving them this information will not endanger Mrs. Janke in any way.

Gaining the older client's involvement at this stage is also facilitated by giving the client an investment in determining what goals will be established. The worker can clearly discuss the expected outcome if goals are reached. When the older client realizes that some change is *possible,* resistance is likely to lessen and involvement to increase. For older clients who have become discouraged about the possibility of their situation ever improving, providing realistic hope can be an impetus in becoming involved in assessment and goal setting.

If elderly clients believe that they have little or no impact on the plans being made concerning them, they are less likely to become involved in this process than if they feel they play an integral role in decision making. Giving the client the clear message that their input is important is helpful to gaining their contribution. With minimal or no involvement at this stage, the older client has no investment in carrying out the goals that are established. The same is true for family members or others who are involved along with the older client.

By ensuring that *trust* exists, providing the client with *hope* that change is possible, and clearly letting the client know that their *participation is not only desired but necessary,* the service provider can gain and maintain the older client's involvement. As human service workers know, change only occurs when clients are willing to become involved and to work at the change process. By gaining their investment and providing them with an incentive to change, the worker has greatly increased the likelihood of the older client's success.

In addition to involving the individual client, the importance of including others significant to the older client in preparing for change must be stressed. Others significant to the client will likely be influenced by the changes that are planned at this stage. When the data gathered reveals the involvement of family members and other significant individuals, it is necessary to determine the elderly client's feelings about including these persons in assessment and goal setting. Too often, significant others are ignored until after goals have been set. As with the older client, the investment of involved others will be facilitated by including them at this stage.

Leonard and Kelly (1975: 115) suggest that when the professional, elderly client, and significant family members join together to assess the client's situation, several benefits result: "(1) it is helpful for the patient [older client] to have people whom he knows and trusts involved in what may turn out to be the plan for the rest of his life; (2) it extends the responsibility and ultimate solution to those most able to assist the patient."

Of course, the client may not be the older person at all, but rather, a family member seeking help in dealing with an elderly relative. Again, the involvement of the client and older family members, throughout all aspects of this stage, enhance the accomplishment of commitment to the goals that will be set.

Determining weaknesses, strengths, and resources. Matching resources to client need involves an analysis of the data gathered. Assessing data from a social systems perspective provides a basis for realizing the specific *needs* that the client is experiencing, the *strengths* of the client, and the resources in the elderly client's *environment.* So that the information gained from assessment can be applied to a plan for bringing about change, an awareness of the potential *resources* to meet needs is also necessary. Information about the elderly client's environment is crucial at this stage as this provides insight as to how needs have developed and are being maintained. This information also presents knowledge about the older client's potential response to the various goals and tasks that must be established in order to achieve desired results.

A social systems approach can facilitate the assessment of needs, strengths, environmental situation, and resources. By examining the older client's linkages with other systems, the manner in which energy is exchanged as well as other aspects of the client as a social system, the human service worker and elderly client will be prepared to set appropriate goals for service delivery. The situation of Mrs. Chambers, discussed in Chapter 5 (Case Example 5.3), will be used as a model for determining needs, strengths, environmental situation, and resources. Readers will recall that Mrs. Chambers was an elderly widow who was referred to an adult day care program by her daughter. Mrs. Chamber's situation will be assessed from a social systems approach.

First, it is helpful to view Mrs. Chambers as a social system, interacting with other social systems. As Mrs. Chambers is the focus of concern for the social worker, she is the primary system. Because of this, it is necessary to examine the other systems with which Mrs. Chambers interacts. Mrs. Chambers is a subsystem of her larger family system, the major system with which she interacts. The other subsystems within her family system include her daughter, Mrs. Sommers (Cynthia), Cynthia's family, and Mrs. Chambers's son Jack and his family. Mrs. Chambers also relates to individuals outside of her family system. She has a relationship with Mrs. O'Neil (her neighbor), acquaintances at the senior citizen's center where she eats lunch once a week, and with the homemaker who helps her weekly. Mrs. Chambers has formed linkages with these social systems and exchanges energy with them.

There is a good deal of information that could be gained concerning the systems with which Mrs. Chambers has linkages. However, the information sought by Miss Gibson (in Case Example 5.3), the social worker, was relevant to the need that *Mrs. Chambers* had expressed: her concern about staying at home alone. The assessment process should also focus on the need perceived by Mrs. Chambers. A service provider could, at this point, decide that Mrs. Chambers and her son should get along well enough so that they could live together. As a consequence, the assessment process could focus on needs related to Mrs. Chambers living with her son. *This is not, however, an issue for Mrs. Chambers.* As noted earlier, older clients have the right to have needs that they have perceived and experienced attended to by the service provider. Therefore, the assessment of information about Mrs. Chambers, her family, and her friends will focus on factors related to Mrs. Chambers's concerns about her fear of being alone at home in the daytime.

It is important to look at the energy exchanges that occur between Mrs. Chambers and the social systems with whom she interacts. It would appear that Mrs. Chambers receives external energy from each of these systems. She has the most frequent interactions with her daughter Cynthia and Cynthia's family and appears to gain significant amounts of energy through her relationships with them. For example, Cynthia provides reassurance, which allows Mrs. Chambers' coping needs to be fulfilled. Cynthia, her husband, and children provide Mrs. Chambers with transportation. This allows Mrs. Chambers to maintain some control over her life, another basic need. In return, Mrs. Chambers expends energy on Cynthia and her family through emotional support (which includes her appreciation of them). It appears, however, that Mrs. Chambers receives more energy from Cynthia and her family than she expends in her relationship with them.

Some external energy is provided to Mrs. Chambers from Jack's family. Support is given at holidays and other family get-togethers. Mrs. Chambers enjoys her relationship with her granddaughters and meets internal goals (in this case, contributory needs) through making cookies for the girls while they are away at college. Both Cynthia and Jack and Mrs. Chambers support one another through discussions of positive times they have had together. This is a source of energy to Mrs. Chambers as it allows her to review her life and continue to perceive it as having been meaningful.

External energy is also obtained through the relationship with Mrs. O'Neil. Mrs. O'Neil shares an affective relationship with Mrs. Chambers and each allows the other to grieve for her husband, as well as to positively review her life. Mrs. Chambers need for friends seems to be strong, and although this is met to an extent through interactions with Mrs. O'Neil, Mrs. Chambers clearly desires to increase her circle of friends. She would like to see her friends from the senior citizens center more often, but lack of transportation limits the opportunity to do so. The energy Mrs. Chambers exchanges with the homemaker is not clearly described in the data gathering session. It would be beneficial to gain more information concerning this. Occasionally, the assessment process highlights the need for more information. Steps should be taken to gain information at any point in the service delivery process where additional data is required.

Mrs. Chambers expends internal energy through worrying about being alone during the day. This expenditure gains little return of energy for her. Although it results in Cynthia's regular involvement, the worrying does create a loss of energy for Mrs. Chambers, as Cynthia cannot always be there for her. Some internal energy is also spent by verbalizing grief for her husband. This may gain energy for her as it allows for some internal organization and helps her to focus on specific concerns and to talk about them. In addition, a function of expressing her feelings about her late husband is the friendship that has developed with Mrs. O'Neil and the apparent strengthening of family ties through discussions about the past.

On the whole, Mrs. Chambers is a fairly well organized social system. There appear to be several areas on which a service provider could focus. First, Mrs. Chambers fear of staying alone seems to expend energy that could be more functional for her if applied elsewhere. This is the area of *need* as perceived by Mrs. Chambers and should be a focus of the goal setting process. Mrs. Chambers has also expressed enjoyment of her lunches at the senior center as well as a desire to see her friends there more often.

Second, Mrs. Chambers appears to have many *strengths*. She utilizes internal energy to form and maintain relationships with others that, in turn, gain her additional energy. Mrs. Chambers also appears to have a history of successfully adapting to change and currently has a willingness to make adjustments that will lessen her fear of being alone. Finally, it appears that resources do exist that can be matched to Mrs. Chamber's needs. The day care center has the potential to provide support for Mrs. Chambers during the day, giving her less to be concerned about. A latent function will be the possibility of developing friendships at the day care center.

If Mrs. Chambers and Miss Gibson assess Mrs. Chambers's situation and decide that Mrs. Chambers will attend the day care center, it is likely that Mrs. Chambers will make the necessary adaptations to accommodate this change. First, she has been involved in the assessment and decision-making process and consequently is likely to be invested in the goals set. Second, she has a history of making successful adaptations to new situations. Third, at the day care center she will meet the need of having someone with her in the daytime. Fourth, based on past relationships, it would appear that Mrs. Chambers has the potential to develop and maintain relationships with other participants at the day care center. Follow-up should involve a reassessment of each of these areas as well as a determination of the needs produced by the changes in Mrs. Chambers's life. The staff at the day care center, with Mrs. Chambers, will need to assess whether the center allows Mrs. Chambers enough private time, enough feeling of control over her life, and if the center provides interests in common with other day care participants.

It would be important to include in the assessment a determination of the toll that caring for her mother has caused Cynthia. Although the day care center will mean fewer worries for Cynthia during the day, her mother will likely want her support to continue in the evening. It would be helpful to determine Cynthia's feelings about this before developing goals that include continued, regular visits by Cynthia with her mother each evening. As noted in the "Values" section of this chapter, it can be damaging to establish goals that prevent others with whom the older client relates from meeting their needs. If visiting with her mother regularly before bedtime demands too much energy from Cynthia, this is unfair. In addition, it will be dysfunctional to the relationship between Cynthia and her mother as, over time, Cynthia will expend more energy than she obtains from the relationship. If this occurs and she does not have other sources of energy to compensate, her energy will be drained and she will have less to exchange with her mother.

Establishing attainable goals. The goals that the human service worker and older client establish must be attainable. If they are not, the elderly·client is likely to encounter failure. The worker can undertake several tasks in order to enhance the possibility that goals can be attained. These tasks involve *establishing limited goals that are small enough for the client to accomplish; making discussions specific; working to encourage those individuals who interact with the older client to support the goals established;* and *determining which resources are clearly a match for the older client's needs.*

The older client or the service provider may become overly ambitious when setting goals to meet needs. If the assessment process has established needs that should be met, numerous goals may come to mind that appear to be ideal. It is important to *limit goals and make them small enough* for the older client to experience success (Herr and Weakland, 1979). Both service provider and client system need to look carefully at possible goals to determine whether they can be met. Brill suggests limiting the areas dealt with is necessary because

problems rarely occur singly or with only one dimension. They are often of such magnitude that they are unmanageable. The number, diversity, and complexity may be overwhelming and may leave the client temporarily unable to act. . . . The worker's responsibility is to assess the totality, help break it down into manageable units, help the client think about and decide where to begin [1985: 194].

The situation of Mrs. Chambers, discussed above, can be utilized to illustrate what can occur when inappropriate goals are set. We will assume that instead of setting an attainable goal, Mrs. Chambers and Miss Gibson could have decided that, based on Mrs. Chambers' concern about being home alone during the daytime, Mrs. Chambers should find friends who could come and stay with her on a regular basis. This goal would likely have been too ambitious, as it would have required Mrs. Chambers to carry out a task that would be difficult to complete. Mrs. Chambers indicated in her earlier interview with Miss Gibson that other than her family, her only close friend was Mrs. O'Neil. She knew other women whom she had met at the senior citizen center's luncheons, but did not feel she knew them well.

The goal of having Mrs. Chambers contact friends to stay with her, if achieved, *would have met her need to have someone with her during the day.* However, because of her limited social network, *it would be very difficult to attain.* If this goal had been established, Mrs. Chambers may have called her acquaintances from the senior citizens' center only to find that they were either not able to stay with her or that they were surprised that someone they did not know well would ask this of them. Even if she were able to find someone to stay with her for part of the time, it would be unlikely that any acquaintance could stay for the hours required to meet Mrs. Chambers' needs. Had Mrs. Chambers and Miss Gibson set this goal, Mrs. Chambers may have felt that she had failed and also that her need could not be met.

A more attainable goal would be to have Mrs. Chambers attend the day care center regularly or to determine the suitability of a system for summoning help when alone. As noted in Chapter 3, some communities provide a service for the elderly that involves wearing a button that, when activated by the older person, summons help from a nearby hospital or life squad agency. As long as the service provider knew that this service was available for Mrs. Chambers and would meet her need, setting the goal of establishing a service of this type would be feasible and would not require more of Mrs. Chambers than she could give.

Setting few enough and small enough goals so that the older

client is likely to succeed will enhance the client's self-concept as well as increase the probability of continued involvement. The service provider and client who set inappropriate goals are likely to meet with failure and consequently reduce the client's willingness to risk continued involvement.

Specificity in establishing service priorities has the function of clarifying for older clients the aspects of their situations that are relevant to the problems at hand and the steps that need to be taken to resolve those problems. The service provider may have a very clear idea as to the procedures that should be followed, but without communication with the older client, the client has no idea about what has happened or why. This prevents older clients from successfully joining in to attain goals as well as denies them the option of developing skills to help themselves when future needs occur. To assure specificity, the service provider should, at each step of the assessment and goal setting, clarify in detail what is being done. Statements too vague or general can prevent the client from successfully learning this stage of the process, as well as lead to misunderstandings in later phases of work with the older client. By the same token, talking to clients in terms they can understand provides more information than does using professional jargon. Again, aged clients require a clear understanding of what is occurring if they are to work toward achieving goals.

Although it has been noted throughout this chapter, the involvement of the aged client's significant social systems during this phase cannot be emphasized enough. If goals are established that *gain the support of the client's significant social systems,* those goals are less likely by be sabotaged during the intervention phase. Individuals not involved in determining if and how change should occur have no investment in facilitating that change. Rather, the proposed changes may threaten them or violate their ability to meet needs. If the elderly client is willing, questioning significant family or others about their feelings concerning appropriate goals will enhance their investment in seeing that those goals are met. If their suggestions are not utilized, the service provider and client should explain to them the reasons for this as well as reasons why other goals were established.

Finally, *goals are more easily attained when the resources that are part of the plan are compatible with older client's needs.* If the resources agreed on during the goal setting process do not exist or are insufficient to meet the client's needs, the client will be unable to succeed in attaining established goals. The service provider can ensure compatibility of resource to need by being aware of what resources exist within his or her community.

The provider also requires complete knowledge of the composition of the resources that are being considered. For example, a system that alerts medical personnel to the fact that a client has fallen (as suggested for Mrs. Chambers, above) can only work if it is likely that the client will be conscious after falling and able to activate the system. A client who faints regularly could not make use of this system. Consequently, the service provider should know how a system of this nature is activated prior to agreeing to make it part of the service plan.

The human service professional also must make sure that desired resources are available for the client with whom he or she is working. For example, a service provider will want to determine whether the client is required to have certain characteristics or to pass a means test in order to qualify for resources, as well as whether there are enough resources to meet the client's needs.

Establishing a contract. As service priorities are established, the older client and individuals who will be providing formal and informal services have the final task of developing a contract. As shown in the sample contract found in the Appendix to this chapter, the contract clearly specifies the goals that have been set and the manner in which those goals will be accomplished. In addition, the contract will indicate to whom responsibilities will be assigned, the dates by which they should be carried out, and the time at which an evaluation of progress should be expected. Maluccio and Marlow (1984: 409) define the contract as

> the explicit agreement between the worker and the client concerning the target problems, the goals and the strategies for social work intervention and the roles and tasks of the participants. Its major features are mutual agreement, differential participation in the intervention process, reciprocal accountability, and explicitness.

The contract is not something that the service provider develops alone and later shares with the older client. Rather, the contract should be "mutually negotiated" (Keefe and Maypole, 1983: 27) as a part of the process of establishing service priorities with the elderly client system. The contract should reflect the assessment and goal setting that has been accomplished between the service provider and older client system and the agreements that have been made between them. During the discussion of the contract, the older client or service provider may realize that they have not understood each other completely. It is valuable to recognize misunderstandings at this point in the service delivery process rather than at a later date.

The contract functions to clarify the specifics of the intervention phase and to prevent expectations from being violated. While it is possible for the contract to be a verbal one, it is advantageous for the human service worker, older client, and others who have accepted responsibilities to share a written statement of the plan for intervention. When the contract is in writing, each individual has a clear indication as to their responsibility and the responsibilities of other parties. This provides older clients with objective information regarding the steps taken to meet their needs.

Also, it is particularly helpful at the time of evaluation to be able to look at the agreement that was made concerning intervention. This will allow all parties to determine accurately the level of success of the intervention efforts. Another function of the written contract is that it makes family members and significant others less hesitant to join in service delivery with the formal service provider as it explicitly outlines each individual's involvement. For relatives who have stated that they want to be involved in helping an older family member, but are hesitant to intrude on formal services provided, a clear delineation of tasks they are expected to perform will encourage involvement in service provision and avoid confusion concerning helping roles.

Finally, the contract can serve as an educational tool. A purpose for working with older clients while establishing service priorities is to educate them about the process of meeting their needs. As noted above, older clients will likely encounter future experiences where needs must be met. The older client will have learned, through experiences with the service provider, how to go about meeting needs. This knowledge can be applied in future problem situations. When this occurs, clients have more control over their circumstances and, consequently, are better able to cope. Of course, it is recognized that older clients may require formal helping services

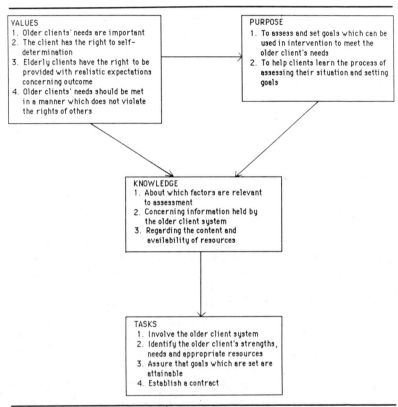

Figure 6.1: Service Provision Framework: Establishing Service Priorities

once they have learned the steps involved in helping themselves. For some elderly clients, formal care will be long term and may last the rest of their lives. However, for all clients, the more they know about helping themselves, the more competent they are allowed to feel and the more self-determining they can be in future situations.

SUMMARY

Establishing service priorities includes assessment as well as setting goals for intervention in the client's situation. This phase of the service delivery process involves a partnership between the older client, the service provider, and individuals significant to the elderly client. The older client's needs, strengths, and situation are assessed and goals are established that make use of available resources compatible to these aspects of the older client system.

In Chapter 7, the process of applying goals to bring about desired change in the older client's situation is discussed. Various modes of intervention will be presented.

APPENDIX: SAMPLE CONTRACT

DATE_____

CLIENT NAME _____

NAMES OF OTHERS INVOLVED _____

_____

_____

GOALS

(1) _____

_____

(2) _____

_____

RESPONSIBILITY OF CLIENT IN REACHING GOALS

GOAL (1) _____

_____

_____

DATE OF EXPECTED COMPLETION_____

GOAL (2) _____

_____

_____

DATE OF EXPECTED COMPLETION_____

RESPONSIBILITY OF SERVICE PROVIDER IN REACHING GOALS

GOAL (1) _____

_____

_____

DATE OF EXPECTED COMPLETION_____

GOAL (2) _____

_____

_____

DATE OF EXPECTED COMPLETION_____

RESPONSIBILITY OF OTHERS (name each and list) IN REACHING GOALS

GOAL (1) _____

_____

_____

DATE OF EXPECTED COMPLETION_____

GOAL (2) _____

_____

_____

DATE OF EXPECTED COMPLETION_____

DATE OF EVALUATION_____

7

DELIVERY OF SERVICES

Service providers who have established a successful relationship with older clients, who have gathered information, and have established service priorities have their work laid out for them. Tasks performed during earlier phases of the service delivery process will, in many ways, direct the activities of the service provider during this phase. However, in addition to the work that the service provider will expect to carry out with the older client, new issues may arise and old issues, believed settled, may reappear. The importance of following through on agreements made with older clients and successfully dealing with issues that undermine the service provider's ability to follow through cannot be underestimated. During this phase, the service provider continues to rely on values, purpose, and knowledge that will direct the tasks carried out in the delivery of services.

VALUES

Service providers intervening in the older client's environment, and in the larger environment, operate with the belief that *older clients have the right to have access to resources that have been determined necessary to meet their needs and to develop their potentials.* In addition, providers will hold the value that *elderly clients should receive those services in a manner that does not demean them, but increases their dignity.* The actual delivery of services can either further the work already accomplished by older clients and service providers or can weaken the ability of elderly clients to improve their situations. The service provider who does not strongly believe that elderly clients have the right to services or who does not view the dignity of older clients as important will have little effect in encouraging the provision of needed resources from other systems or in motivating the older client to make adjustments necessary to improve his or her situation.

The right of older clients to have access to resources. Elderly clients have the right to resources that meet their needs and develop their potentials. During the service delivery phase, this value has a slightly different meaning than in earlier stages of work. As the practitioner actually engages in the delivery of services, this value motivates the provider and *results in advocacy,* when needed, for the older client. Advocacy involves "working with and on behalf of individual clients or families to assure that they receive benefits and services to that they are entitled and that the services are rendered in ways that safeguard the dignity of the recipients" (Hepworth and Larsen, 1986: 504).

Advocacy for older clients requires that service providers believe strongly enough in the older client's right to receive resources that an active effort will be made to help the client attain them. Case Example 7.1, below, presents a situation in which the service provider herself lacked the belief that the client had the right to receive specific resources. The older client in this situation required services for her physical and emotional well-being; however, the service provider did not advocate for the client to receive those services.

Case Example 7.1

Mrs. Techman was the evening nurse on duty at a nursing facility in a small midwestern town. Just that day, the physician who consulted with the facility had berated the nursing staff for making numerous "unnecessary" calls to him during the evenings concerning the physical complaints of the residents. One nurse had called the evening before to request an order for medication that had already been ordered by the physician. The physician stated that he only wanted to receive emergency calls in the evenings.

This particular evening, Mrs. Techman was approached by the son of an elderly frail resident, Mrs. Bundy. Mrs. Bundy's son told Mrs. Techman that his mother was experiencing pains in her chest. He requested that she call the physician immediately. After a brief examination of Mrs. Bundy, Mrs. Techman reported to the son that she believed his mother only had "heartburn." She said that a nurse would call the physician in the morning if the pain continued.

Mrs. Bundy's son called the physician himself and explained his mother's symptoms. The physician came to the nursing facility immediately and had Mrs. Bundy transported to a hospital. Mrs. Bundy had experienced cardiac arrest.

In this situation, Mrs. Techman was more concerned about the possibility of incurring the consulting physician's wrath than she was about the rights of her client. Had she actually believed that Mrs. Bundy had the right to receive resources necessary for her well-being, Mrs. Techman would have examined Mrs. Bundy more thoroughly and would have called the physician advocating for Mrs. Bundy. The provider who actually believes in an elderly client's right to receive needed resources will strive to do away with barriers to those resources. This value is strengthened by the belief that *older clients have the right to maintain trust in the service provider.*

Trust, which has been established throughout the earlier stages of work together, will either be strengthened or weakened during this phase. If the service provider and client have established realistic goals and followed through on these, the older client's trust is likely to be increased. However, if the goals that were set are impossible to attain or if the service provider is not reliable in carrying out agreed upon tasks, the elderly client may feel that trust in the provider is unwarranted.

Clients who have lost faith in the service provider will have difficulty involving themselves in gaining access to services or in utilizing those services once received. Consequently, the belief that older clients should be able to maintain trust in the service provider is an integral part of the belief that older clients have the right to receive services.

Value of retaining older clients' dignity. Services provided to the elderly can either enhance their sense of dignity or decrease it. The service provider who values the dignity of older clients will be more successful in providing services and will allow the elderly client to function more effectively during the professional relationship and after it has ended.

Retaining the older client's dignity, at this stage, involves *continuing the partnership established with the client* during earlier stages, working to *help other social systems that are providing resources to treat the client in a dignified manner, following through on commitments made to the older client,* and *maintaining an awareness of the client's individuality.*

The older client's dignity may be lessened if the service provider disregards the *partnership* that the two had established earlier. During this stage, joint efforts between the practitioner and client are particularly important to the older client's self-concept. As was noted earlier, older clients' participation in providing information and in setting service priorities is important to their self-determination and, consequently, to their dignity.

Expecting clients to be involved up to the actual delivery of services, but not to enter in actively at this stage, gives a clear message about the service provider's perceptions of the client's capabilities. For the frail elderly client, partnership may involve different activities than it would with a vigorous older person. However, the attitude of desiring the older client's involvement and the action of utilizing that involvement to the greatest amount possible function to maintain the older client's dignity. The benefits of valuing older client self-determination and partnership are illustrated in Case Example 7.2.

Case Example 7.2

Mr. Mitchell was a 78-year-old widower whose physical health had declined in recent years. Until the age of 72, Mr. Mitchell had owned and operated his own business. His business had been quite successful and he had taken pride in his financial accomplishments. When he had sold his business, he had looked forward to the opportunity of traveling with his wife of 50 years. However, Mrs. Mitchell died within a year of her husband's retirement.

Mr. Mitchell continued to live in the home that he and his wife had shared. He became actively involved in relationships with his grandchildren. He managed household tasks, often had grandchildren stay at his house overnight, and continued social activities in his community. At the age of 76, Mr. Mitchell developed problems with his vision and was involved in several minor car accidents. During that year, his family noticed that he had less energy than before. Following a severe chest cold, his children encouraged him to move to a retirement facility near his home. Mr. Mitchell's children were worried that he would become involved in a severe accident if he continued to drive or that, in his weakened condition, he would fall and suffer injury if he continued to live alone. Although Mr. Mitchell was not anxious to leave his home, he agreed to his children's request and added his name to the retirement facility's waiting list.

Upon admission to the retirement facility, Mr. Mitchell took an active interest in furnishing his room with items from his home. The staff of the facility felt that he was making a satisfactory adjustment. Mr. Mitchell was surprised when his two sons told him that they felt they should handle his finances. Although Mr. Mitchell was experiencing no difficulty in managing in this area, his children believed that, because of his age, he would soon become "senile." Anxious to avoid conflict with his children, Mr. Mitchell agreed to give his sons control of his finances.

Mr. Mitchell found himself with little to do at the retirement facility. He no longer had a home to manage, meals to cook, or a car to drive. His grandchildren visited him occasionally, but his relationship with them differed from their previous relationship. When they visited, there was little for them to do in the facility. They could not stay overnight as they had in their grandfather's home. Their visits now consisted of making polite conversation with their grandfather instead of joining in activities together with him as they had previously done.

Mr. Mitchell felt less competent than he had felt before. He realized that his children viewed him as being old and helpless. Upon losing control of his money, he felt that he no longer had activities that allowed him control over his life. Mr. Mitchell began to focus on past experiences that had been pleasurable to him. He talked about the future without enthusiasm. He became less involved in activities for residents of the retirement facility. He began to have difficulty sleeping, ate less than he previously had, and on occasion appeared to be confused. Several of the staff members became concerned about Mr. Mitchell and referred him to the facility's social worker.

After meeting with Mr. Mitchell and gathering information from him and from his family, the social worker and Mr. Mitchell decided to work together to find meaningful activities in which Mr. Mitchell could engage. In addition, Mr. Mitchell had expressed a desire to resume control of his checkbook and bank accounts. He and the social worker had agreed that he would share this desire with his sons.

After Mr. Mitchell and the social worker had set goals together, Mr. Mitchell did not become active in working toward those goals. The social worker realized that Mr. Mitchell expected her to act on the goals that the two of them had set. This expectation partially developed out of Mr. Mitchell's recent experiences with his children, in which they had taken over responsibilities for him. In addition, Mr. Mitchell was depressed. He felt he had little control over his life and was uncertain about his ability to regain control. The social worker expressed to Mr. Mitchell her belief that he could carry out the tasks that they had agreed on. She suggested that he begin with one of the smaller tasks: finding an activity that he would enjoy within the retirement facility. Mr. Mitchell met with the activities director and talked about different activities in which he could participate. He discovered that once a month there was an activity for residents and their grandchildren. He decided to invite a grandchild to this and did so, with the support of the social worker.

The task of confronting his sons about regaining control of his financial affairs was much more difficult for Mr. Mitchell. He requested that the social worker talk to his sons for him. The social worker stated that she could meet with him and his sons, but she wanted him to address his concerns to them. The social worker told Mr. Mitchell that when he discussed his feelings with his sons, she would talk with them about his ability to handle his checkbook and bank accounts and that she would provide them with information about the aging process and the fact that the majority of older individuals continue successful intellectual functioning.

The social worker and Mr. Mitchell met with his sons and talked with them as they had agreed. The sons were surprised to learn that their father wanted to and was able to handle money matters. They agreed to return this responsibility to him. As Mr. Mitchell gained more control over his environment, he viewed the future more positively. His appetite increased and sleeping problems diminished. The confusion that occurred during his depression no longer occurred.

The social worker involved in Mr. Mitchell's situation valued his participation in their work together. She clearly indicated that she expected their relationship to be a partnership during the service delivery stage. When Mr. Mitchell was uncertain about joining in to gain the resources he needed, the social worker began by having him carry out small tasks in which he could be successful. Through her support, the social worker provided external energy that allowed Mr. Mitchell to become a partner with her, gain access to desired resources, and redevelop his feelings of dignity and control over his environment.

Service providers can help older clients retain dignity when they enable *other resource systems to value the client's dignity.* Regardless of the respect the service provider shows elderly clients, lack of respect by others with whom clients interact regularly will influence the clients' feelings about themselves. When practitioners can act to increase the ability of other involved resource systems to treat older clients with dignity, older clients will benefit. Specific tasks that employ skills to help clients retain dignity will be discussed in the "Tasks" section of this chapter.

Service provision enhances the dignity of elderly clients when *service providers follow through on commitments made* to those clients. Practitioners who fulfill their responsibilities as agreed on at the time of the contract allow the older client to feel that the practitioner believes them to be worthwhile. Delivery of resources that violates the expectations that clients have been led to believe are realistic cannot help but demean clients.

Finally, retaining the older client's dignity involves *treating the client as an individual.* This requires maintaining an awareness, throughout the service provision stage, that the older client is a unique individual with a unique set of circumstances. For example, it is vital to remain aware of the older client's traditional pattern of responses, family history, and ethnic background. At this stage, as well as during other stages, it is necessary to recognize that these aspects do not determine behavior but may provide information about the client. A minority family, for example, may share characteristics with other families who are part of that minority group, but also exhibit differences from those families. The following statement suggests that this is true for Mexican American families:

> In speaking of the 'traditional' Mexican American family, one must realize that the heterogeneity of Mexican Americans . . . means that generalizations based on such a label must be made with caution. . . . The 'traditional' family type . . . refers to a family pattern that is different from what may be considered the prevalent or 'typical' Anglo pattern [Alvirez et al., 1981: 273].

All older adults exhibit characteristics or have experiences that give clues about behaviors to explore, but the uniqueness of each client must still be attended to. An awareness that each client is unique and attention to cues from information gained about the client will facilitate human service professionals in viewing older clients as individuals. Without this perspective, the service provider may violate the dignity of older clients.

PURPOSE

The purpose of service delivery is derived from the values of the service provider. During this phase of service provision, human service workers will strive to ensure that services are provided that match resources to need. The dignity of elderly clients is validated when they receive resources that allow them to meet their needs and reach their potentials. At this phase in the service delivery process, matching resources to need involves attention to service delivery priorities that have been set, determination as to whether those priorities continue to be appropriate, ensuring that services that are provided are consistent with the priorities, and enabling clients to appropriately utilize the resources that are available.

KNOWLEDGE

As the older client and practitioner operationalize the goals that they have established together, interactions with other social systems will probably take place. In order to match resources to the needs of the older client, the practitioner will use knowledge about social systems, about elderly individuals, about the particular older client to whom services are being provided, and about the specific social systems involved with the older client. This knowledge has been gained in earlier stages. In addition, knowledge specific to this phase is also required. Service provision calls for (1) *knowledge about delivery of services to elderly clients*, (2) *knowledge about establishing and maintaining linkages with resource systems*, as well as (3) *knowledge about how to interact with other resource systems as an advocate* for the elderly client.

Knowledge about delivering services to elderly clients. Knowledge about service delivery to elderly clients involves *maintaining a positive relationship* with older clients, knowing how to *continue client self-determination*, as well as having information about the *interactions of older clients with the social systems related to them.* If practitioners lack knowledge, older clients may not make the adaptations necessary to benefit from resources or may even terminate the professional relationship at this stage. Knowledge about how to deliver services successfully will strengthen the service provider's linkages with older clients. In addition, knowledge in this area can serve as a source of internal energy to the practitioner, facilitating the practitioner's provision of energy to the older client.

In order to *maintain a positive relationship with older clients,* the service provider requires knowledge about keeping the client's trust, which was gained in earlier phases of the service delivery process. Keeping the client's trust involves employing values. This requires knowing how to enhance the older client's dignity by continuing the client-service provider partnership while delivering services. The older individual who participates in the service delivery process is much more likely to have confidence in the work being done and in the relationship with the service provider.

Another factor in maintaining trust is viewing the older client as an individual. The importance of this value has been noted above. Knowledge about how to accomplish this requires attention to information gathered at the beginning of the service delivery process as well as a constant awareness of the client's needs, feelings, and experiences throughout the process. Trust is also maintained by following through on commitments made to the older client. At the time service priorities were established, the service provider and client made commitments to one another about the tasks that would be carried out. The service provider who fails to act as agreed upon will lose the client's trust during this phase.

Knowledge about delivering services to elderly clients involves having information about *how to continue client self-determination* while services are delivered. As partnership is necessary to maintaining the older client's trust, it is also vital to continuing client self-determination. Knowledge about facilitating client self-determination through partnership during this phase involves information about factors that motivate individual clients. Some aged clients may be motivated by their circumstances to seek outside help and to go through the process of setting goals with the service provider, but may lack the motivation to carry out the agreed upon tasks. To gain information about the client's movtivation, it may be necessary to reopen a discussion with the older client about the results desired and the client's willingness to participate.

Knowledge about continuing self-determination is also enhanced by gaining information about the internal and external resources (energies) available to the older client. It may be that the elderly client lacks the resources necessary to become an actor in actual process of obtaining services. This could be related to the client's organization of available resources and/or to internal conflicts or conflicts with significant others. Consequently, *information about how the client and related other social systems are expending energy* during this phase is also important. If exchanges of energy are not productive, the client will have difficulty adapting to the resources that are being provided.

Knowledge about establishing and maintaining linkages with resource systems. Delivery of services to elderly clients will involve developing relationships with other social systems. The human service worker will relate to these systems during the delivery of services and so may the elderly client. In some situations, the service provider may have already established relationships with resource systems during earlier phases of the service provision process, while the client may have had ongoing relationships with resource systems for an even longer period of time.

Information about other resource systems with services related to the older client's needs will have been gained in earlier stages. During this phase, the practitioner will want to know how to best approach those systems. If positive relationships have already been established with those systems, the service provider will want to involve them in meeting current goals. This is most beneficial when carried out in a manner that enables those systems to become invested in the older client's welfare.

If negative relationships exist between the service provider and needed resource systems, the provider will require knowledge about how to focus on current concerns without resurrecting past, problematic issues. If the older client and resource systems have had negative interactions, the practitioner will need information about past relationships. In that situation, knowledge is needed about whether functional relationships can be reestablished and about other resource systems that could more successfully deliver services.

Once relationships with resource systems have been established, their maintenance is aided by information about how other systems perceive the practitioner, the older clients, and the service priorities that have been established. Also, knowing how to exchange energy successfully with other resource systems is beneficial. This includes knowing how to communicate in a way that those systems perceive as being helpful to them and to their work with the older client. Effective communication with relevant resource systems and the elderly client also involves knowledge about case management.

Knowledge about advocacy. Knowledge about maintenance of relationships contributes to the practitioners' *information concerning how to serve as advocates for their clients in interaction with other resource systems.* Also contributing is knowledge about advocacy itself. Advocacy, as noted above, calls for work that attempts to do away with barriers to resources needed by clients. Advocacy may also include attempts to gain resources for individuals or for larger groups of people through trying to change social policy (Hepworth and Larsen, 1986). Knowing how to advocate with various types of systems for client needs is important. The knowledge that practitioners have concerning service delivery must be utilized if goals are to be met. In carrying out tasks, service providers integrate values, purpose, and knowledge and utilize skills to match resources to the needs of the individual client with whom they are working.

TASKS

During this phase, the service provider and older client work to actualize the plans that they have developed. In order to accomplish this, several tasks will need to be carried out. Each task that the service provider enacts successfully requires skill. The tasks of the service provider include (1) *enabling older clients to gain access to resources,* and (2) *working to ensure that services are provided to elderly clients in a manner that enhances their dignity.*

Enabling older clients to gain access to resources. The task of enabling older clients to gain access to resources involves several smaller tasks. First, the service provider will *maintain the trust that has been established with the aged client.* Second, the provider will need to *establish and maintain linkages between older clients and resource systems.*

The importance of *maintaining clients' trust* during this phase has been discussed above. One of the tasks of maintaining trust involves *reliability* on the part of the service provider. The elderly client and service provider have agreed on the plan of action that will be taken. The service provider has, in earlier stages, clearly explained to the client the responsibilities of each. The older client, then, has been led to believe that the service provider will take part in specific actions in order to accomplish the plan that was established. If the practitioner, for whatever reason, does not fulfill the responsibilities promised, the client will not view the service provider as credible. This is important in work with all older clients and particularly important for those older clients who have few systems on whom they can depend, other than the service provider.

Reliability requires that service providers be organized in their work with older clients. The service provider's ability to carry out agreements reliably with the older client will be increased by making notations concerning agreements with the client, setting dates by which work will be accomplished, and regularly reviewing case notes to determine tasks that should be completed.

Achieving *open communication* is another task that contributes to the ability of the client to trust the worker. If the professional regularly communicates with the client about the progress of their work together, misunderstandings are less likely to occur. A latent function of open communication is that it enhances the older client's perception of the worker as being reliable. If the practitioner is, for some reason, unable to follow through on commitments made to the client, open communication will provide the client with information concerning this and the reasons for the lack of follow through.

A third task that helps to maintain the older client's trust is regular *evaluation*. Evaluation should be an ongoing procedure during the time that services are being delivered. Both worker and client should regularly evaluate their progress, their satisfaction or dissatisfaction with the work completed, and their perceptions as to whether the goals that were originally established were appropriate. If the evaluation results in negative findings, worker and client will want to determine appropriate steps to take. Case Example 7.3 describes a situation where this has occurred.

Case Example 7.3

Mr. Dalton, an 80-year-old man, had met several times with Mrs. Gerdin, a medical social worker. Mr. Dalton was hospitalized and his physician had recommended that he not return home but move to a long-term care facility. Mrs. Gerdin and Mr. Dalton had agreed on this and had established a contract in which each party had responsibilities to carry out.

Mrs. Gerdin's responsibilities included contacting several long-term care facilities in order to determine whether they had Medicaid beds available. Mr. Dalton's responsibility was to talk with his son about this and to respond to information that Mrs. Gerdin would provide following her contacts with nursing facilities.

After contacting several long-term care facilities in their area, Mrs. Gerdin returned to Mr. Dalton to provide him with the results of her contacts. Three facilities currently had Medicaid beds available (more than Mrs. Gerdin could usually locate). Mr. Dalton stated that he did not want to live in any of these facilities, although he had not seen them and knew little of them. Mr. Dalton had not spoken to his son about the physician's recommendation, as he had previously agreed to do.

Mrs. Gerdin suggested that she and Mr. Dalton discuss the goals and responsibilities that they had agreed on. During the discussion, Mr. Dalton revealed that he felt he had been pushed by his physician into agreeing to institutionalization. He stated that he was not sure how he felt about not returning home, but that he had not had enough time to think about being discharged.

Mrs. Gerdin, requested a meeting with Mr. Dalton, his son, and the physician to discuss Mr. Dalton's feelings as well as to reevaluate the goals that had been originally established. Mr. Dalton agreed to this. During the meeting, Mr. Dalton expressed his concerns about moving from his own home. He said that he did not understand why he needed to do this and that he knew too little about the long-term care facilities in his area. The physician restated his reasons for the recommendation that he had made, Mr. Dalton's son described again to his father the reasons why Mr. Dalton could not live in his home at this time, and Mrs. Gerdin told Mr. Dalton the information she had about the nursing facilities that currently had openings.

Even though Mrs. Gerdin had followed through with the responsibilities she had agreed on, open communication and evaluation were also necessary to help Mr. Dalton trust her enough to reveal his concerns. These concerns had not been shared in earlier meetings and were important to discuss, if Mr. Dalton was to have access to the resources that he needed.

Trust in the service provider allows the older client to remain a partner in the service delivery process and to utilize the services that are available. If trust does not exist, older clients may feel that others have control over the actions that are being taken rather than feeling that they are in control of their own lives.

The act of *establishing and maintaining linkages between clients and resource systems* involves advocacy, case management, and education. Each of these tasks will help the practitioner develop and maintain functional relationships between older clients and resource systems. This task is essential if resources are to be matched to the needs of elderly clients.

Advocacy for an older client requires, as noted above, information concerning the needs and desires of the older client as well as the situation of the systems with whom the worker is advocating. Advocating without thorough knowledge of the needs and desires of older clients may result in clients not being treated in a dignified manner. It is important not to take a paternal stance in advocating for older clients and not to assume that what the practitioner "knows" is best for the client is in fact best. As Gambrill (1983: 295) suggests, "One error you will have to guard against is thinking that you know, better than people themselves, what they want." One way to guard against this is to communicate with the older client concerning the practitioner's work as an advocate and to include clients in advocating for themselves to the extent that this is possible.

The result of communication with and involvement of the client could be that advocacy is curtailed. Older clients have the right to be self-determining, and "if clients do not wish to assert their rights, practitioners are ethically bound to respect their wishes" (Hepworth and Larsen, 1986: 571). To exemplify, a nurse in a long-term care facility may be aware that an older resident feels badly because her daughter seldom visits her. In discussing this with the resident, the nurse offers to ask the daughter to visit her mother (as the resident is physically unable to make telephone calls or to write). The resident, however, indicates that she does not want her daughter to be contacted. In this situation, the nurse must respect the resident's right to be self-determining and allow the resident to maintain control in this area of her life.

When advocating for older clients, practitioners need to take into consideration *the situations of the individuals to whom they are relating.* The systems with which the service provider is advocating may be unable to provide resources for the older client. For example, Cicirelli (1983) found that adult children whose marriages were "disrupted" did not provide as much help to their aged parents as did adult children with "intact" marriages. It may be that the stresses and problems that the adult children experience preclude them from becoming involved with their parents to the extent that adult children with intact marriages do. The service provider who advocates with adult children with disrupted marriages to provide more help to their parents may only frustrate and overwhelm the children and disappoint the older parent when help does not result. Analyzing resource systems from a social systems perspective will provide information about the potential success of advocacy with them.

As noted earlier, a situation may also exist where a potential resource system and older client have had negative experiences. When this occurs, the service provider will need to seek information about the previous relationship. Advocacy may take the form of communicating with the resource system and client so that understanding can be reached and relationships bettered.

Service providers are more successful in advocating for their older clients when they have already worked to establish positive relationships with a variety of potential resources. Case Example 7.4 reveals that effective advocacy may depend on relationships with other systems that were developed prior to the current situation.

Case Example 7.4

A caseworker in a state psychiatric hospital had developed good relationships with nursing staff members on the geriatric unit. When one of the caseworker's clients in the geriatric unit requested a weekend pass to visit his son, the head physician let it be known that he planned to veto the request when it was discussed at an upcoming team meeting.

The physician stated that the resident's son should not have to be "bothered" with his father, and that the father would not benefit from the visit because he was disoriented. Because the caseworker knew that the son wanted his father to visit and believed that the visit would be beneficial to the father, she decided to advocate for her client. The caseworker began by talking with the nurse (who would attend the team meeting) about reasons for supporting the patient's request and asked the nurse to support the request at the upcoming team meeting.

The nurse stated that although she did not think the visit would do the older resident "any good," she did not think that it would harm him either. She agreed to support the resident's request out of respect for the caseworker, based on their previous relationship. As a result of the strong support for the older resident's request, the physician agreed to sign a weekend pass for him.

The caseworker's effective advocacy for the client in Case Example 7.4 was facilitated by a positive relationship with the nurse as well as by a direct request for her support. Service providers who have earned the respect of other professionals will find advocacy an easier task than those who have not. In addition, practitioners who have provided energy to other resource systems in the past may find that those systems are willing to reciprocate in the current situation.

Advocacy for some older clients may require undoing stereotypes held concerning older clients or a specific group of older clients. For example, a service provider working with a minority elderly client may encounter individuals who present barriers to needed resources because of the stereotypes that they hold. When this occurs, it is the service provider's responsibility to advocate for the minority client, as well as to provide education to the biased individual. This task must be carried out successfully if the older client is to receive services that maintain dignity, as exemplified in the following case example.

Case Example 7.5

Mr. Adson, a social worker in a Department of Human Services in a large eastern city, was assigned to work with an elderly, frail Puerto Rican man, Mr. Garcia. Mr. Garcia had lived with his daughter and her family for a year. The housing arrangement had been satisfactory for all concerned. However, Mr. Garcia could no longer walk alone and had become incontinent of urine. His daughter and her husband felt that they could no longer care for him in their home.

When Mr. Adson contacted a long-term care facility to inquire about Mr. Garcia's admission there, the business manager indicated that a bed was available. However, when the business manager was given Mr. Garcia's name, he became less cooperative. He commented that he was not anxious to admit a Puerto Rican male as "they are irresponsible freeloaders."

Mr. Adson reminded the facility's business manager that it was illegal for him to refuse admission to an individual because that individual is a member of a minority group. He also described to the manager Mr. Garcia's background, informing him of Mr. Garcia's excellent work record and of his responsible care for his family over the years. He stated that Mr. Garcia's background was not unique for Puerto Ricans, but typical in many Puerto Rican families.

Once Mr. Garcia was placed in the long-term care facility, Mr. Adson continued to follow-up on his status, visiting him at first and forming a positive relationship with the social worker in the facility. Mr. Adson did not terminate his relationship with Mr. Garcia until he was assured that Mr. Garcia was not being discriminated against as a resident of the facility.

In the case example above, Mr. Adson advocated for Mr. Garcia in an open manner. He left the business manager with no doubt that he was concerned about his client and that he would stand up for his rights. He also provided information to the business manager that indicated that his client did not fit with his stereotype about Puerto Ricans, and that the business manager's stereotype could not be successfully be applied to other Puerto Rican individuals.

Case management is a method of maintaining linkages between older clients and resource systems. Case management involves arranging for services with formal and informal service providers and coordinating the provision of those services once they have begun. "An important aspect of case management is connecting the client with appropriate resources and ensuring that she utilize these resources effectively" (Gambrill, 1983: 296).

The practitioner who is a case manager for an older client may be coordinating the services of others while also providing some services to the client. Once the contract is established with service providers and client, the case manager will need to make regular contacts with both service providers and older clients to determine whether the client is receiving the agreed upon resources. The case manager will also need to make note of how the various resource providers and older client are exchanging energy and adjusting to the relationship with one another.

In addition, the case manager requires an awareness that unplanned situations may occur. For example, a family member of the older client may become threatened by changes in the client. If this occurs, the family member could strongly advise the client to discontinue relationships with various resource systems. A case manager who is alert to potential problems will be better able to respond to them when they occur.

Education is another task involved in forming and maintaining linkages between older client and resource systems. Open communication, as described above, is a way of educating clients and resource systems about the situations of each. It may be that older clients will require education concerning the utilization of resource systems. For example, an elderly client who has been hospitalized and is returning home with an oxygen unit may need education from the hospital nursing staff about how to use that unit successfully. Without education, the nursing staff might not be effective in linking the client to the medical social worker whose job it is to plan with the client for discharge, as the client's fear of using oxygen may cause resistance to discharge planning.

Provision of resources that enhance the older client's dignity. The importance of maintaining and enhancing the elderly client's dignity at this stage has been discussed above. One of the tasks involved in accomplishing this is to *involve the older person as a partner* throughout this phase. In addition, *helping other systems provide services in manner that retain the client's dignity* is a task of the practitioner. A third task is to *provide education for the purpose of preventing future difficulties.*

As has been emphasized, delivery of services to older clients does not denote a passive client who receives services from an active worker. Rather, *effective delivery of services involves a partnership between service provider and older client.* Clients who are active in gaining resources are more successful in meeting expressive and contributory needs. Older clients have agreed, when priorities were established, to the responsibilities they would undertake. Ongoing evaluation, regularly completed, between clients and practitioners will continue to remind clients of the expectation that they are capable of carrying out their responsibilities.

If clients become less involved during this phase, it is important to determine the reasons for this and to deal with them. Older clients who have little physical energy may, during this phase, decrease their involvement. An awareness of this, and flexibility on the practitioner's part, can allow practitioner and client to find new, less demanding ways in which the client can continue involvement.

Decreased involvement may also occur because family, fictive kin, or formal agencies have extended their involvement beyond the level that was agreed on. This can be the result of a desire to help the older person, but may have the opposite effect. The service provider's task, then, is to help these systems respond to the older client in a manner that will enhance his or her dignity. This may involve helping the overzealous systems to gain insight into the effects of their behavior or may call for direct confrontation.

Working with other systems to preserve the older client's dignity may, at times, be difficult. Practitioners will encounter individuals, frequently professionals, who hold stereotypic beliefs about the elderly or about particular racial groups, as noted in Case Example 7.5. Although the practitioner may be unsuccessful in doing away with stereotypes, educating those individuals about the characteristics of the specific client with whom they are working will help ageist and racist professionals to treat the client in a dignified manner. In addition, those professionals may apply knowledge gained from this experience to other experiences with other elderly clients.

The service provider may also encounter individuals who rob the elderly client of dignity through physical or emotional abuse. Because the majority of abuse to the elderly is instigated by family members, the service provider may be the only individual outside of the family system who is aware of that the abuse has occurred. When there are physical signs of abuse (facial cuts, bruises in different stages of healing, fractures), the service provider is ethically and may be legally responsible to report the abuse to the appropriate authorities. Communication with the suspected abuser to discover the reasons for abuse and to provide support to that person can indirectly help the older, abused client. Treating the suspected abuser with anger may prevent that person from responding to the older client in a positive way.

In striving to facilitate other systems in treating the older client with dignity, it is beneficial to be alert to the fact that others may not view the older client with respect, to model respect for the older client and to support those individuals who lack the information necessary to treat the older client with dignity.

Finally, *educating clients* as to how to engage other systems in service delivery and how to respond to the receipt of services will help clients accomplish this independently when problems occur in the future. Educating clients indicates a belief that the client is capable of understanding the work being accomplished and is capable of some degree of independence. This belief, when put into action, will enhance the dignity of the older client.

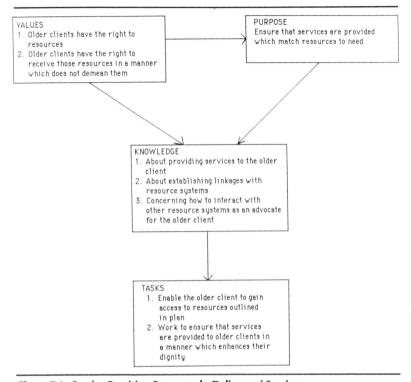

Figure 7.1: Service Provision Framework: Delivery of Services

CONCLUSION

It is vital for service providers to apply the values, purpose, and knowledge of this stage to the tasks that are carried out for and with elderly clients.

An awareness of the social systems with which the older client is involved and an analysis of the interactions between those systems and the primary client system provide information necessary to successful intervention with elderly clients. When this is accomplished, the service provider can more successfully enable older clients to gain resources in a dignified manner. As a result, fewer barriers to clients meeting basic coping, expressive, contributory needs, as well as the need to maintain control over their situations, will exist.

8

EVALUATION AND TERMINATION

Evaluation and termination are aspects of the final stage of service delivery to elderly clients. In work with the elderly, these stages are often overlooked and not built into the service delivery process. However, they are vital components of work with aged clients. Successful completion of this phase allows the older client to learn from the experience with the practitioner and to incorporate knowledge gained into future interactions with others. Without a successful, explicit ending to the relationship, older clients are not allowed the opportunity to experience the degree of independence that they could otherwise attain. Of course, some elderly clients will continue to require the human service worker's involvement throughout their lifetimes (Butler and Lewis, 1982). When this is true, the older client and practitioner still can gain from regularly scheduled evaluations.

Evaluation and termination are presented together because aspects of the two overlap, creating one phase of work with the older client with two distinct parts. Within this chapter, evaluation and termination with elderly clients will be described. Following this, the values, purpose, knowledge, and tasks of this stage will be delineated.

EVALUATION

Evaluation of the work completed between older client and service provider examines the goals originally established and judges whether these goals have been accomplished (Brubaker, 1983). Evaluation is a continuous process that will occur throughout the time that services are provided (Compton and Galaway, 1984). Each meeting with the elderly client should include an evaluation of the work completed between and during sessions. Regular evaluations remind both worker and client that there is a purpose for their relationship, as well as inform them of the progress of their work. In addition to continuous evaluation, a summary evaluation of the service delivery process and of the outcome of that process is a separate stage of work with the client.

Evaluation with elderly clients is important for several reasons. First, it provides information about the success of intervention with the client. Second, it allows the service provider and client to determine the value of the service provider's input into the change process (Pinkston and Linsk, 1984). This is necessary information for the service provider planning to work with other older clients. Third, evaluation gives input as to the influence that the change process has had on other social systems involved with the older client. If other social systems have difficulties as a result of the changes made in the older client's life, the service provider and older client must deal with this.

The fourth reason for carrying out an evaluation is educational. It reminds older clients of the steps involved in creating change. Finally, evaluation is necessary if elderly clients are to maintain the changes accomplished. As will be discussed in the "Tasks" section below, both evaluation and termination are geared to enable older clients to continue successfully to meet their needs.

TERMINATION

Termination refers to the end of the professional relationship between older client and practitioner (Edinberg, 1985). Termination is not merely tagged onto the end of the process of work with older clients. Termination is important to the clients' future actions as it can shape older clients' perceptions of their ability to deal with present and future problems successfully. In addition, the service provider who handles termination well can facilitate the older client's approach to other endings he or she will encounter.

Termination of work with elderly clients can occur for a number of reasons (Brill, 1985; Lowy, 1985). The ideal termination results when the client has achieved success in attaining the goals that have been established. Elderly clients may also terminate the relationship if they perceive that it is unsuccessful. This perception may be realistic or may result from fears about the changes that will be required of them (as discussed in Chapter 6). In addition, others significant to the older client may also encourage termination because they resent the practitioner's involvement or because they are concerned about what the suggested changes will mean in their own lives. The professional relationship may also be terminated when the older client moves to a different location or when it is more appropriate for another service provider to become involved with the client. For example, an adult service worker in a county department of human services may have developed a relationship with an elderly woman, but terminate that relationship when the woman moves to a long-term care facility and services are referred to the social worker there. Termination also occurs when the older client dies. Termination includes ending the relationship with the older client *as well as with others involved in the service delivery process.* Family or others significant to the older client may have time and emotional investment in the relationship with the service provider.

As human service workers and elderly clients evaluate and terminate relationships, they rely on values, purposes, knowledge, and tasks. Successful completion of this stage can prepare older clients to respond more successfully to their environments and to gain control over their situations in the future.

VALUES

Two values that will facilitate the service provider in successfully completing work with the older client are (1) the value that older clients must be treated with dignity; and (2) the value that older clients should be allowed to be self-determining. These same values have been discussed in earlier chapters concerning other stages of work with older clients. What do they mean in terms of evaluating and terminating work with older clients at this stage?

Treating the older client with dignity. To treat aged clients with dignity at this stage requires a belief that clients are individuals who respond in different ways. Each client will respond to evaluation and termination in a characteristic manner. For some clients, lack of success in achieving some goals will not overly concern them. These clients may focus on the successes they have accomplished and ignore the fact that there is still work to be done. Other clients will be unable to view themselves as successful to any extent and will see themselves as failures despite what has been accomplished. One elderly client may view an evaluation of the work completed as threatening while others may be stimulated and challenged by the evaluation process. When terminating, some clients may have difficulty in ending the relationship with the service provider (Brill, 1985) while others may be glad to be done with this phase of their lives (Epstein, 1980).

Treating the older client with dignity requires a *sensitivity* to how the client is likely to respond at this stage, an *acknowledgment* of the client's right to respond in his or her own characteristic manner, and an *attempt* to work with clients to accomplish successfully this phase based on their needs. Case Example 8.1 illustrates how an older client's feelings can be recognized and responded to appropriately.

Case Example 8.1

Mr. Smithson, a 69-year-old individual, had been meeting for two months with Mrs. Frances, a social worker at a senior citizens' center. Their relationship had been initiated by Mr. Smithson, who had asked if they could talk regarding his concerns about his wife's illness. Mr. Smithson was anxious to have nursing and housekeeping help in the home. In addition, he indicated that he was having difficulty in adjusting emotionally to his wife's illness and requested that Mrs. Frances talk with him concerning this.

As a result of their meetings, a visiting nurse and homemaker began coming to the Smithson's home regularly. Mr. Smithson reported that this arrangement was satisfactory, as it met his and his wife's needs. In addition, Mr. Smithson had accepted his wife's illness and had adjusted to this satisfactorily.

Mrs. Frances enjoyed her meetings with Mr. Smithson. She appreciated his willingness to work toward reaching the goals they had set and his flexibility in dealing with the problems that he encountered. At the time of termination and evaluation, she shared these feelings with him. However, she was aware that although Mr. Smithson appreciated their relationship, termination would not be difficult for him. He accepted that his efforts had been successful and was anxious to spend his time in other ways. As a result, Mrs. Frances ended the relationship by allowing Mr. Smithson to feel successful, sharing with him the strengths that she saw him to possess and letting him know that she was available if future needs should arise.

In the example above, Mrs. Frances could have spent a good deal of time telling Mr. Smithson that endings are difficult for most clients, conveying the expectation that termination of their relationship would be troublesome for him as well. However, this would have led Mr. Smithson to believe that Mrs. Frances did not know him well after all, or that she was patronizing him. Instead, she did not detract from his dignity by assuming that he was feeling something that perhaps the majority of her clients feel. In addition, Mrs. Frances did not inappropriately burden Mr. Smithson with her feelings about the relationship. Epstein (1980: 257) suggests, "A practitioner may provoke unhappiness in a client about termination if the practitioner has overvalued the relationship and if the excess valuation has been communicated to the client by word and deed." Unsuccessful termination may occur because of the practitioner's "hangups about endings" (Gambrill, 1983: 357), while successful termination is facilitated by attention to the client's feelings during this stage.

In another situation, with an older client or older family who had become dependent on the worker, it would be imperative to talk about the difficulties that they were experiencing in ending the relationship. To ignore their sorrow about or fear of termination would deprive them of a dignified ending to the relationship and perhaps make them feel foolish for their feelings.

By maintaining or enhancing the older client's dignity in the final stage of the professional relationship, the service provider will help older clients gain a sense of control over their environments. This will be beneficial as the client attempts to maintain the changes that have been accomplished during the course of the relationship with the service provider.

Self-determination. Older client self-determination in evaluating the professional relationship involves the client taking an active role in reviewing and judging the degree to which goals were achieved and the reasons for success or failure in each area. Client self-determination in terminating the relationship calls for the client to talk about ending the relationship, discuss feelings, and be *actively* involved in saying goodbye to the service provider. The partnership between elderly client and service provider continues throughout this stage.

The elderly client's right to self-determination is particularly important to this stage. In encouraging older clients to be self-determining during evaluation and termination, the service provider is reinforcing behavior that has been established and that will, it is hoped, continue after the relationship has ended. The elderly client or older family who is asked to play an active role in evaluating the success of attaining goals and in terminating will better know how to evaluate and end other efforts and relationships in the future.

In addition, it is important that the service provider clearly points out, at this stage, that the client has been self-determining throughout the process of their relationship (if this is accurate). If any success has been achieved, it is necessary for clients to own their part in that. Older clients who feel that they can achieve success are much more likely to attempt to solve problems in the future. Those individuals who believe that successes are the result of the service provider's efforts will likely question their ability to succeed in other situations they encounter.

If, on the other hand, older clients have not been successful in meeting goals, it is important that they take responsibility for the part they played in this *as well as for any small successes that were achieved.* Service providers may want to spare clients because they are older. However, this makes a statement about the providers' perception of the clients' ability to succeed. The older client who is too frail to be faced with the reality of the evaluation was likely too frail to have embarked on the change effort. In situations such as this, it will probably be a family member or a significant other who is the client. These individuals, too, deserve to take part in an honest evaluation of their efforts.

In treating older clients with dignity and allowing them to be self-determining, the service provider reinforces work that has been accomplished and facilitates the clients' ability to maintain changes.

PURPOSES

The service provider has two purposes at this stage of work with older clients. Both the practitioner and client must *determine if the goals that were established have been met.* This will involve a review of the goals that were set originally as well as of the process undertaken in reaching those goals. If the goals have not been successfully accomplished, the older client and practitioner will want to establish a new purpose for their work together, as will be discussed later in this chapter. If goals have been achieved and no further goals are established, the provider and client will attempt to terminate the relationship in a manner that *maintains the changes that have been accomplished.* To accomplish these purposes, knowledge is required and tasks must be carried out.

KNOWLEDGE

To achieve the purposes described above, practitioners require knowledge about: (1) *how to carry out evaluations with older client systems;* (2) *how to end relationships;* and (3) *how to facilitate older clients in maintaining changes that they have accomplished.*

Knowledge of evaluation. To evaluate the elderly client, the practitioner requires knowledge about the following: the *steps* involved in the evaluation process; how to discuss goals set, actions taken and results accomplished in *specific and clear language;* and *how to gain the older client's active involvement* at his stage.

In proceeding with *the steps of evaluation,* the practitioner will need to know how to discuss the contract in order to determine whether goals have been met. Knowledge about how to decide whether to continue working on goals, set new goals, or end the relationship will also be required. The "Tasks" section of this chapter will provide information about specific steps to take.

Knowledge about successful communication is valuable in reaching an understanding about the results of work with the client. For example, in evaluating the success of their relationship, a social worker could ask the client, "Well, how did you think things went? Do you think we need to continue meeting?" The response from the client would likely be as vague the worker's questions. When the practitioner lacks knowledge about how to use specific and clear communication with the client, the relationship may end without a thorough evaluation. As a result, the practitioner may not recognize that problems have not been resolved to the older client's satisfaction. When the service provider has knowledge about how to be go through the steps of evaluation using specific language, this stage is more likely to be successfully completed.

The practitioner with knowledge about *gaining the older client's investment in the evaluation process* also facilitates success at this stage. As noted, involvement in evaluation can increase self-determination on the part of the elderly client. Clients may lack awareness either about what evaluation involves or about what their participation should include at this stage. Knowing how to provide the older client with information concerning this is needed to involve successfully the older client in the evaluation process.

Knowledge about ending relationships. As noted above, ending relationships with elderly clients calls for *knowledge about the individual client's feelings* concerning the relationship. In addition, *information is needed about how the aged client responds to terminating relationships in general.* If the older client has learned how to end relationships successfully with others, the practitioner will respond differently than if the older client has a history of withdrawing or feeling rejected when relationships end.

Ending relationships is difficult for many people. For some, patterns of dependent interactions keep them inappropriately tied to others. Throughout their lifetimes, individuals attempt to maintain a balance between independence from and dependence on other individuals.

> Human relationships are characterized by a process of being together and of being apart from one another. Two strong emotional forces are at work in this process: the need for emotional closeness, which brings people together; and the desire for the individuality and autonomy, which moves the individual away from the control of others [Janzen and Harris, 1986: 16].

Some elderly clients will have resolved the conflict between dependence and independence. These individuals will have learned how to establish linkages with others that allow them to maintain boundaries permitting a functional exchange of energy with others. These older persons can interact with others without trying to control them and without losing control over their own lives. Other elderly clients will not have gained this level of independence. For these persons, dependency will likely characterize their relationships. Ending relationships with others will be threatening for them.

The extent of "personal investment" in the relationship is another factor with potential to influence the client's response to termination (Brill, 1985: 110). As Edinberg suggests,

> Termination can be difficult for both the older client and mental health practitioner. Because the relationship may be one of few if any where there is intimacy and trust, termination can represent another irreplaceable loss for the client [1985: 148].

If the service provider has been the elderly client's major source of external energy, termination will have a much different meaning than if the older client interacts successfully with other systems.

For the majority of clients, numerous factors will influence their response to termination. The interaction of these factors may create ambivalent feelings on the part of the client. As a result, many clients may approach termination with conflicting feelings (Hepworth and Larson, 1986: 33).

Because of older clients' different responses to ending relation-ships, the end of the professional relationship will not be the same for every client. For those elderly clients who can end the professional relationship in a productive way, there are certain advantages. Epstein (1980: 257) points out that for clients, termina-tion can have many benefits. These include "more money in the pocket (if the client is paying a fee), more time, more indepen-dence." For other clients, however, these advantages will not compensate for the loss of regular meetings with the service provider. To deal successfully with different responses to termina-tion, the service provider must *know how to end relationships with different types of clients.*

Finally, the provider needs *an awareness of his or her own feelings about endings.* A lack of self-awareness can cause the provider to project personal feelings onto the older client and, as a result, respond to the client inappropriately. Also, the practitioner may encourage the client to be dependent because of a lack of self-awareness (Okun, 1982), particularly in this phase of work.

Knowledge about maintaining change. Setting the stage for the older client to maintain progress and for continuation of resources is a necessity if the relationship is to be considered successful. Consequently, practitioners will want to *know how to help older clients believe that they have been successful and can succeed in the future, when this is realistic.* Older clients need to have confidence as they proceed without the involvement of the service provider. However, the practitioner must also *know how to prepare the older client for possible failures and difficulties that will likely be encountered after the relationship has ended.* The client who believes that the work accomplished in the professional relationship will prevent future problems may become discouraged when difficulties occur.

Maintaining success and preventing future problems is also facilitated by the service provider's *knowledge about how to review the process in a way that educates the older client.* The value of educating clients has been discussed in earlier stages. It continues to be a necessity at this stage, as well. Knowing how attempts to meet needs can be evaluated and how to end relationships will be important to the client in the future.

Finally, *knowledge is needed about how and when to follow up on older clients* after regular meetings have ended. In some cases, follow up will only continue a dependent relationship. In others, follow up is necessary to determine whether the resources provided earlier continue to be available and appropriate. Older persons may need the continued involvement of the service provider (Butler and Lewis, 1982) as needs may continue or recur with regularity. The elderly vary as much as does any age group. Some frail elderly individuals may require regular follow-up visits or calls while this may be inappropriate for other vigorous, aged persons. Consequently, knowledge of when and how to follow up with an older client is helpful in maintaining change.

TASKS

The tasks of evaluation and termination will employ the values, purposes, and knowledge of the human service worker. As worker and older client evaluate the possibility of terminating their relationship, they will carry out the tasks of (1) *reviewing the service delivery process and outcome;* (2) *determining the steps to be taken, based on the findings of the review;* (3) *developing a framework to maintain change, if change has occurred;* and (4) *ending the relationship, if that is appropriate.* Each of these tasks requires a partnership between the elderly client and the service provider, as well as with other involved individuals. In addition, each task will be carried out in a manner that may serve to educate the client regarding how to evaluate and end relationships in the future.

Reviewing the service delivery process and outcome. The major task of review is to *examine the goals established, the steps that were taken to reach those goals, and the outcome of the efforts made.* Review of the work completed by the older client and service provider involves a *joint effort* by the two, as well as the involvement of other individuals who participated in this process. The service provider will also want to *communicate clearly* with the client.

In order *to review the process and outcome* of work with the older client, the practitioner should be prepared with a copy of the contract that was established earlier in their relationship. In addition, the practitioner and client will want to ask any individuals who were part of the contractual agreement to meet with them. Review should have been an ongoing activity, carried out each time the service provider and client have met. Consequently, the older client and provider have regularly refreshed their memories concerning agreements originally made and have noted successes as well as areas of work requiring improvement. However, at this point, a summary evaluation will take place that involves an examination of the entire process and of the final results.

The tasks to be carried out during the summary evaluation include a discussion of the goals that were established during the priority setting phase. Goals ideally will be considered one at a time, with the individuals participating in the review making a decision as to whether each goal has been achieved. After the outcome of a goal has been decided, it is valuable to look at the process that was involved in bringing about the results. *The practitioner will want to elicit the opinions and ideas of all the individuals attending the evaluation session.* As the discussion takes place, a task of the practitioner is to keep the conversation *specific and focused.* It is during the review that clients often indicate *feelings about ending work* with the practitioner. Successful communication skills allow the practitioner to respond to both verbal and nonverbal messages concerning this.

Determining steps to be taken. Following the summary evaluation itself, certain steps will be taken depending on evaluation results. If evaluation of outcome indicates that goals were met *and* that the older client and significant others are satisfied with the current situation, then termination is indicated. At this point, the service provider and older client have the task of terminating the relationship.

If the client wishes to work on new goals, then the service provider and client must determine whether this is appropriate or if the elderly client has suggested additional goals as an attempt to continue the relationship. It may be that the older client does not require continued services, but is having difficulty in ending the relationship. Should the client's wish to work on new areas with the service provider be appropriate, the provider and client will gain any additional, relevant information, establish new service priorities, and follow with intervention and evaluation.

If the elderly client's reason for suggesting new goals is related to the older client's fear of functioning without the service provider, the provider must work with the client concerning this issue. To determine the client's reasons for wishing to continue, the practitioner can call on information gained throughout the service delivery process.

It may be that ending relationships is difficult for the client. By enabling the older client to deal with ending this situation appropriately, the service provider may facilitate the client's ability to face successfully the ending of other relationships. This is particularly important for older clients, who face the termination of relationships when elderly friends and family die. Service providers can help clients deal with the end of this professional relationship by expressing their own feelings about the relationship being completed. For example, a service provider can express, "Mrs. Smith, I feel that we have come to know one another quite well. I'll really miss seeing you each week, but I will remember you and the work that we did together." By expressing feelings, the service provider gives the client permission talk about how he or she feels regarding the end of their relationship.

If continuation is needed because the outcome goals have not been met, it is helpful to determine whether the process itself prevented this or whether the original goals established were unattainable or inappropriate (Pincus and Minahan, 1973). If someone involved in the service delivery process did not fulfill their responsibilities, as agreed on when the contract was established, a discussion should take place as to what prevented this. The discussion about the goals that were not achieved should be handled openly and in a "noncritical way" (Thorman, 1982). Following this, a new agreement can be made as to tasks that will be carried out by each party. It may be that responsibilities were not completed because they were too difficult or because the client was not involved enough in the early stages of the service delivery process.

On the other hand, agreed on tasks may have been carried out, but did not accomplish the desired results. In this case, tasks that were established should be reviewed and it may be appropriate to establish new tasks to meet the desired goals. When new goals or tasks are established, it is not as though the service provider and client are beginning a new relationship. Rather, they have a history of working together and may have developed a strong, positive relationship or both may feel a sense of failure at not having accomplished what they wished. If a sense of failure exists, the service provider will want to view the experience as an educational one for him- or herself and the client, as well as to reestablish trust with and a realistic sense of confidence in the client. In future situations, the older client may not experience success in attempts to deal with problems. The knowledge gained from this situation can facilitate future attempts to cope.

Developing a framework to maintain change. Older clients who have made progress during the service delivery process may or may not maintain that progress once the professional relationship has been terminated. However, there are actions that the service provider can take to reinforce the changes that have been made and to help the older client be ready to handle future difficulties successfully. These actions include *involving significant others, planning for the future, anticipating potential problems, and allowing the client to feel success.*

One of the most important aspects of maintaining change is *involving others significant to the older client* (Gambrill, 1983). If this has been done throughout the service delivery process, it is much easier to do in the evaluation and termination phase. Individuals significant to the older client might include family members or other friends of neighbors with whom the older client has a close relationship. Other persons important to the client could include formal caregivers, such as a homemaker/home health aide, a visiting nurse, or the nursing staff in a long-term care facility.

It is hoped that the other client's situation will have improved as a result of the services that have been provided. If the individuals who are involved with the older client have not been included in the evaluation, they may not be aware of the improvements accomplished. As a result, they will have little reason to support them. In addition, significant others are less likely to be threatened by changes in the older client or in the older client's situation if they have been made to feel that they are a part of those changes. Case Example 8.2 indicates the value of involving significant others in evaluation.

Case Example 8.2

Mrs. Atcheson, age 81, resided in a long-term care facility. Her husband, who had visited her regularly, had recently died. Mrs. Atcheson had difficulty in accepting his death. The only way in which she would express her grief was with verbal anger toward the nursing staff and by refusing to become involved in any of the facility's activities.

The social service worker in the facility had met with her over a period of time to help her verbalize her grief appropriately. As Mrs. Atcheson became able to talk about husband's death, she expressed feelings of guilt and also anger that he had died. She felt guilty because she wondered if having to visit her so often had been a physical strain for him. She was angry that he had died before she had, as he had always been the healthier of the two and she had expected him to outlive her.

As Mrs. Atcheson verbalized her grief and worked through her feelings of guilt and anger, she was less hostile to the nursing staff and more able to join into relationships with other individuals in the facility. Both she and the social service worker were pleased at her progress and decided to end their regular meetings together.

Mrs. Atcheson's daughter, who visited the facility on a weekly basis, was not informed about the progress her mother had made. When she visited her mother, she was uncomfortable with discussing her mother's feelings about Mr. Atcheson's death. She told her mother that she did not want to discuss this and hoped that her mother would not tell anyone that she had felt either angry or guilty about Mr. Atcheson dying, as few people would understand. In the daughter's following visits she reinforced these statements and Mrs. Atcheson become less open at the facility and less involved with others there.

Had the social service worker in the above case example asked Mrs. Atcheson's permission to contact her daughter, she could have at least shared with her the progress Mrs. Atcheson had made and perhaps even asked for the daughter's help in encouraging her mother to continue to express her grief as needed. If this had occurred, the daughter may have felt that she was an important part in her mother's adjustment to the death of her husband and have encouraged her mother to maintain her progress. In addition, the daughter herself may have benefited from talking about her father's death.

Making *specific plans for future action* is also helpful in maintaining change. Part of the termination process should include a plan for the future, when the client does not have regular access to the service provider (Golan, 1986). If an older client has a plan of action for the future, the ending of the present relationship may seem less overwhelming. A planned, structured future is certainly preferable to a nebulous one for most individuals. In addition, planning for actions to take and work to accomplish can lend a feeling of anticipation to ending the professional relationship.

A plan for the future can be in the form of a contract between the service provider and the older client or can involve a verbal discussion about what the client will do after the relationship is ended. Either way, it is helpful to clearly outline the actions older clients will take to enhance their situations and the activities that will be carried out by others to facilitate the older client. For example, it might be decide that, following the termination of a relationship between a social worker and elderly client, the older person will carry out some responsibilities, a formal service agency (such as a visiting nurse agency) would continue services already being provided, and family members would visit with the elderly person on a regularly established basis. The plan for furture action should involve the full participation of the older client and any other individuals who will be involved.

The plan for future activities may involve structured follow-up by the service provider. The advantages of follow-up have been discussed above. When possible, follow-up should be planned and the reasons for it discussed with the older client. If not, when the service provider becomes involved again, older clients may feel that the provider has lost confidence in their ability to succeed or the client might become unrealistically hopeful that the professional relationship will be reestablished.

Part of planning for the future will involve a discussion of *potential problems that can occur for the older client after termination.* Older clients will encounter difficulties after the professional relationship has ended. The less surprised they are by problems, the more able they will be to handle them. Herr and Weakland (1979) suggest that the service provider describe some potential problems to the older client and ask the client to think of how they could handle those difficulties. Another approach would be to ask the clients themselves to think of difficulties that they might come across. This could bring up hidden concerns that the client has not discussed before.

One of the most important tasks in maintaining the change that has been effected is to *allow clients to feel success for the work accomplished.* Without a belief that they can be successful, older clients may become discouraged after the professional relationship has ended. Older clients have come into the professional relationship with a characteristic way of viewing themselves. Some elderly clients feel they have achieved little in their lives and are not capable of accomplishing anything worthwhile. For these individuals, success in the work they have accomplished within the service provider-client relationship can be used to develop their feelings of self-worth. It is likely that these clients will downplay their successes and focus on their failures. By specifically pointing to the achievements attained by the client (or to the areas in which the client worked hard to meet goals that were established) and discussing how achievements were accomplished, the service provider can provide the older client with a perception of having attained some success. However, it is important to acknowledge the areas where desired results did not occur. Otherwise, older clients will not believe that the professional is sincere about acknowledging their achievements. Clients will disregard patronizing praise, while sincere regard for accomplishments is a source of external energy for the older client.

Ending the relationship. Terminating the relationship with the elderly client is a task that requires skill on the part of the service provider. A successful termination can help to prepare the client for future activities. Without a feeling that the relationship has ended, the client may have difficulty initiating independent actions. Brill (1985: 152) states,

> If the helping relationship is at all significant, the way it ends will be important in terms of the client's self-image and capacity for future relationships. The reasons for termination should be clear in the minds of both client and worker and, whenever possible, feelings about it expressed and understood.

Ending the relationship with the elderly client requires the service provider to *plan* for termination, *determine the older* client's feelings regarding termination, attend to others significant to the elderly client, and work toward self-awareness regarding termination.

Preparation for termination of the professional relationship should begin with the establishment of a contract and continue throughout the relationship. Consequently, preparation does not just happen, but results from an active *plan* developed by the practitioner and elderly client. At the time when the contract is developed, it is helpful to decide approximately how many times the service provider and older client will meet together. It is helpful for the service provider to talk, at this point, about the fact that the relationship will end (if in fact service provision is not expected to continue until the death of the older client). When discussing progress during meetings with the client, it is advantageous to talk about progress toward termination.

The importance of *determining the older client's feelings regarding termination* has been discussed above. Carrying out this task involves several steps. First, service providers will want to be aware of older clients' levels of dependence or independence throughout the service delivery process. If older clients attempt to depend on the service provider during the various stages of the relationship, as in Case Example 8.3, they are more likely to have difficulty separating from the service provider at the time of termination. The client may also have given clues concerning feelings about separation during discussions of termination throughout the relationship.

Case Example 8.3

Mrs. Schroeder, a 68-year-old widow, had been meeting with Mr. Morton, a counselor at the community mental health center for two months. Mrs. Schroeder had originally come to the mental health center following her husband's death. She had been very dependent on her husband and was concerned that she would be unable to handle the responsibilities of daily living without him.

Mrs. Schroeder and Mr. Morton had agreed to work toward Mrs. Schroeder gaining the skills and confidence to face life without her husband. At the beginning of the relationship, Mrs. Schroeder attempted to depend on Mr. Morton rather than to carry out the responsibilities she had agreed on. She often asked Mr. Morton to make decisions for her. As the relationship progressed, Mrs. Schroeder became more confident and made fewer attempts to depend inappropriately on Mr. Morton. However, anytime Mrs. Schroeder faced a situation that she perceived to be a crisis, she would try to have Mr. Morton take over her responsibilities. When Mr. Morton refused to do this and supported her as she worked toward independence, Mrs. Schroeder experienced success.

When the time for termination came, Mrs. Schroeder stated that she felt she was not ready to end their relationship. She indicated that she still needed Mr. Morton to make decisions for her. Mr. Morton pointed out that he had not made any decisions for her and that she had been making decisions on her own for the past two months, as their joint evaluation had just indicated. The two discussed the fact that ending relationships can be frightening and talked about different ways Mrs. Schroeder could deal with this.

In this case example, Mrs. Schroeder had become more independent, but was not ready to give up her attempts to have other people take responsibility for her. She had a lifelong pattern of interacting with people by being dependent and had learned to gain energy through this. Even though she obtained energy from Mr. Morton for being independent, she continued to perceive herself as the dependent person in the relationship. Mr. Morton, however, refused to allow her to maintain this illusion and insisted on having her recognize the numerous times when she had acted independently.

Many clients will develop some dependence on the practitioner, and this is not necessarily harmful (Epstein, 1980). In Mrs. Schroeder's situation, however, the *extent* of dependence she sought with Mr. Morton would not have been helpful to her. For those elderly clients who lack other resource systems, the service provider will be one of the few individuals on whom they can depend. It is the service provider's responsibility to help those clients initiate interactions with other resource systems prior to termination.

Mr. Morton could see throughout the relationship that Mrs. Schroeder was attempting to depend excessively on him. Although he did not allow this to occur, he was supportive of Mrs. Schroeder. If Mr. Morton had agreed to continue the relationship so that he could make decisions for Mrs. Schroeder, he would have been supporting her dependence. It would be very appropriate, however, for Mr. Morton to suggest to Mrs. Schroeder that they meet once more, two weeks later, and that he call her once every two weeks for the following month. Follow-up can be a step in the termination process that serves to provide continued energy when needed, as well as to ensure that necessary resources are still being provided.

If older clients have indicated an excessive dependence on the service provider, the service provider will want to suggest activities that will increase the client's independence. If clients show a reticence to discuss termination when it is brought up, the provider should not avoid the topic. Rather, clients benefit from an open discussion about endings and their feelings concerning terminating the relationship with the practitioner.

It is also helpful to have information about the client's history of ending other relationships. All individuals develop patterns of interaction. These patterns will be applied in various relationships with others. If older clients have had a difficult time separating from individuals in the past, ending this relationship may be hard for them as well. Some older persons may never have learned to end relationships successfully and, consequently, lack the skills required to successfully end the relationship with the service provider. With an older client who has not learned to end relationships successfully, the service provider can model how to accomplish this satisfactorily, as well as allow the client to *experience* the termination process. Service providers are a positive model when they are comfortable with termination, can verbally express their feelings about ending the relationship with the client and support the older client in ending the relationship. As service provider and client go through the steps of planning for termination, the client is gaining experience in dealing with separation while receiving support.

Termination with an older client may also signal the end of a relationship with *others significant to the client.* If other individuals have been involved in the relationship with the elderly client, their relationship must be acknowledged. This not only serves the purpose of maintaining change, as discussed above, but also helps the significant others end a relationship that may have been important to them. Family members or others involved wih the older client may have come to appreciate the service provider's support and be concerned about ending the relationship. They, too, need to work through the process of termination with the provider.

For some families, it may be the death of a loved one that brings about the end of a relationship with a service provider. To end a relationship with family members immediately following the death of an elderly individual may prove harmful. Families who have experienced the death of an elderly member may require the continued involvement of a service provider in

> working through their loss and in achieving a new equilibrium. By virtue of the close ties that have been maintained between families and institutions in the care of the elderly, the abrupt severing of relationships on the day of death or the funeral is experienced by families as uncaring, as bureaucratic, as abandonment [Solomon, 1983: 94-95].

When an elderly client has died, continued involvement with families should be investigated and a termination plan developed with them.

Service providers who are uncomfortable with death may prefer to avoid families at this time, just as providers who do not deal well with termination might wish to avoid talking about ending a relationship. *However,* this will not meet the needs of older clients or of others significant to them. *Service providers may be meeting their own needs rather than those of their clients unless they become aware of their own feelings about termination.* The service provider who is aware of feelings concerning the ending of relationships is better prepared to focus on the needs of the client. Okun (1982: 78-79) states that gaining self-awareness is facilitated by asking oneself these questions: (1) "Am I aware . . . when I find myself feeling uncomfortable with a client or a particular subject area?" and (2) "Am I aware of my own avoidance strategies?" We cannot expect our older clients to terminate successfully if we ourselves cannot do this.

SUMMARY

Evaluation and termination both are important aspects of the final phase of work with elderly clients. Throughout this phase,

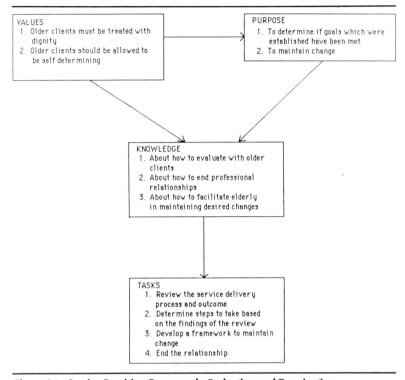

Figure 8.1: Service Provision Framework: Evaluation and Termination

human service workers will attempt to involve the older client and others significant to the client in a review of work completed, as well as to prepare them for the end of the professional relationship. When this is accomplished, elderly clients are better prepared to cope successfully with other situations that they will encounter.

9

FUTURE DIRECTIONS FOR SERVICES TO THE ELDERLY

Several themes have been focused on throughout this book. These themes have been discussed in relation to the *various stages of the service delivery process*. An emphasis has been placed on applying *values, purpose, and knowledge concerning older clients to the tasks* that the service provider carries out. In addition, *utilizing a social systems perspective* when working with older clients has been explained and stressed. Finally, the importance of *working with elderly clients to meet their common basic and individual needs* has been presented. This chapter will present a brief review of these themes, followed by an examination of future directions for services to the elderly.

REVIEW

Service providers engaged in work with elderly clients form a relationship with those clients. The relationship between service provider and client is a *process* that must be attended to if it is to be successful. The process of the relationship involves several stages. First, service provider and client initiate a relationship. This stage forms a foundation for the remainder of the relationship between the service provider and client system. Success during this stage will facilitate carrying out the remainder of work with the client. Difficulties that occur as the relationship begins must be dealt with if future service delivery is to be successful.

As the relationship begins, the service provider and older client work to gain information concerning the client and the other social systems with which the client is involved. Gathering information about the client is a distinct stage of work. However, it is also an ongoing activity that overlaps with other stages, beginning with the first client contact and continuing through termination.

After data concerning the older client have been gathered, the client and service provider, *together,* establish priorities for service. This stage is influenced by the preceding stages and is central to the remainder of work that will be carried out. Establishing service priorities involves both an assessment of the information that has been gathered and setting goals for the services that will be provided.

The actual delivery of services is directed by the goals that have been established as well as by the relationship that has been developed between the service provider and older client. The term "delivery of services" does not imply that a service provider gives services to an older client, but rather that the client and service provider work together to ensure that required services will be obtained.

Following the delivery of services stage, the elderly client and service provider evaluate the service delivery process. The goals that were established and the tasks that were carried out are examined to determine whether the client's needs have been matched by the resources gained. If the evaluation indicates success in matching resources to needs, and if no other services are apparently required at this time, the relationship will be terminated. Termination is important to the future, successful functioning of older clients and must be treated as a stage in its own right. If the client's needs have not been met by the services provided, then a review should be undertaken to determine the appropriateness of the goals that were established and the success of the work carried out.

At each stage of the service delivery process, the service provider is guided by *values, purpose, knowledge, and tasks.* Service providers each hold values concerning providing services to older clients and these values influence the services that they provide. General values concerning service provision become more specific and differ somewhat at each stage of the service delivery process. Values influence the purpose of service provision. The service provider's values and purpose(s) function to direct the knowledge sought and used by the provider. For example, a service provider who values client self-determination and whose purpose is to match appropriate services to needs will seek and rely on knowledge concerning involving the older client and determining needs and resources available. In contrast, a service provider who prefers to meet the client's needs without the client's involvement is more likely to seek knowledge about how to be successfully directive with the older client.

Values, purpose, and knowledge all have an impact on the tasks that are chosen by the service provider. Tasks must be skillfully employed if they are to be carried out in a manner that meets the client's needs. In addition, tasks are most successful when enacted in partnership with the older client.

Throughout this book, the importance of using a social systems approach has been stressed. Older clients are not isolated individuals; they influence and are influenced by those with whom they interact. Ignoring the social systems that directly and indirectly relate to older clients can disrupt the possibly tenuous balance that has been achieved by a client. Viewing the client from a social systems perspective provides the human service professional with information about strengths and weaknesses that will influence the older client's ability to obtain and utilize necessary resources.

Older individuals each have individual needs, as well as more general needs such as the need to cope, the need to express themselves, the need to contribute to themselves and to others, and the need to maintain control over their environments. Older clients are facilitated in meeting each of these general needs when service providers allow them and expect them to participate as a partner in the service delivery process. Obviously, all older clients cannot participate to the same extent. However, clients who are encouraged to become involved to the greatest extent possible are the most likely to meet their general as well as individual needs.

Throughout the book, work with older clients has primarily been approached from a direct service perspective. Service providers who apply the information provided must also be aware that they will encounter societal influences that will influence their work with older clients. These influences often come in the form of social policies and funding.

FUTURE DIRECTIONS

The future of service provision to the elderly will be largely influenced by policies and funding directed toward human services. As cutbacks continue to occur in funding social services for the elderly, attention to the areas emphasized throughout the book will facilitate human service workers in planning and carrying out work with older clients. Regardless of available funding, elderly clients continue to require social services. In fact, as funding for social services to the elderly decreases, various private resources may be tapped to provide for the needs of older individuals. Resources lacking some sort of centralized coordination can lead to services that are more fragmented. As gaps in services widen, some elderly individuals who could marginally function with the aid of human service providers will not be able to continue to live independently once available services have been depleted or become inaccessible.

For example, an elderly individual may be able to remain in the community in her own home with the help of a visiting nurse, a homemaker and an adult service worker. However, when decreased funding to the formal service agencies involved with the client limits the services available to her, she may be unable to continue to live successfully in her own home. The adult service worker may find that his caseload has increased as elderly clients' needs multiply due to the lack of formal services. Consequently, he will have less time to help her find a solution to the problems she is experiencing. If other formal services are unavailable to this woman, and family help is not sufficient to meet her needs, this older woman may not receive the services or attention she so badly needs.

Human service workers burdened with large caseloads and overwhelming client needs may be tempted to meet minimal, immediate needs of elderly clients rather than attending to the long-term effects of their relationships with them. Shortcut approaches to work with the elderly result in a lack of attention to process. In attempting to meet an immediate need of a client as quickly as possible, it is easy to forget that *some sort of relationship is being formed.* If the service provider's actions are not directed toward gaining the older client's trust, the client's needs may not be met satisfactorily. Or, if the service provider has numerous other clients to meet with, applying the value of self-determination and meeting this older client's need of gaining some control over her situation may be neglected. It may be easier and faster for a service provider to carry out activities without the client's involvement, but the result can be damaging to the older client.

How can service providers respond to changes in the social service arena in a manner that will allow them to work successfully with older clients? There are several activities that direct service workers can carry out for this purpose. Service providers can *advocate* for their clients, *work toward making the client's environments more responsive* to their needs, attempt to *provide case management* for their elderly clients, and become involved in *education and research.*

Advocacy. Advocacy for older clients has been discussed in earlier chapters. Advocacy can take place for an individual client who experiences a need *or* for a group of elderly clients. When an older client requires services that are not developed or are not available, the service provider will want to become involved, with the client when possible, in advocating for the delivery of those services. In an era when some social services are scarce, a number of the service provider's elderly clients may experience a lack of access to certain needed services. When this occurs, the service provider has the responsibility to advocate for the provision of those services as needed by that group of clients.

Advocacy requires the older client's approval and is strengthened by the client's involvement. Advocacy may take place for an individual client or for a larger number of clients. When a group of elderly clients' experience a need, discussing advocacy with them and encouraging them to join in the process of advocating for themselves has several functions. Advocacy can be an educational experience for the older client. Involving those elderly who have experienced inflexible environments in advocating for services can educate them about their rights to have needs met, about the fact that other social systems can be expected to be responsive to them, and about how to influence their environments. The success of elderly individual advocating for themselves is exemplified by the Gray Panthers and their advocacy for issues related to the elderly.

The task of advocacy should flow directly from the service delivery process and should make use of basic human service values, purposes, and knowledge. Advocating for older clients' can result in increasing their ability to meet basic needs. When advocacy results in the provision of required services, the external energy available to the older client is increased. And when advocacy reflects the application of human service values, purpose, and knowledge, the older client's ability to utilize that energy is respected and enhanced.

A human service provider who accepts that services cannot be increased and as a consequence, does not advocate for changes in the older client's environment, gives the older clients the message that they will have to make all the adjustments. This violates the right of older clients to be self-determining and prevents them from gaining control over their environments. Kosberg (1976: 80) substantiates this, stating, "Often self-determination and human dignity are denied this group [the elderly]. For example, lack of alternatives to institutionalization make mockery of the notion of self-determination." In addition, acceptance, by direct service workers, of limited or unsatisfactory resources for older clients denies policymakers the opportunity to respond to the needs of clients. As Taubman (1985: 180) suggests, "minimizing the negative effect of massive budget cuts may lull the profession and its communities and legislatures into the complacency of thinking that less is more."

Advocates for elderly clients need information about how to form linkages with and intervene in social systems in the larger environment. Dear and Patti (1981) assert that successful advocacy requires knowledge and they suggest guidelines for advocating within legislative systems. Advocacy within any system will be more effective when the advocate understands how the system operates, knows what forms of advocacy have been successful in the past with that system, and recognizes the goals of that system.

Facilitating the environment's responsiveness. If practitioners are to advocate successfully for their elderly clients, they must be in contact with individuals who determine policies and develop programs influencing the elderly population. "Policymakers need to be alerted to the necessity of establishing better lines of communication with program administrators and other service professionals" (Nofz, 1986: 90). Policymakers cannot be alerted to this necessity unless direct service providers advocate for their older clients and provide information that will allow for the desired responses.

Attempting to make the larger environment responsive to the elderly client is necessary if resources are to be matched to need. *Too often, the needs of older clients are matched to available resources.* In other words, older clients are expected to make the adjustments and to ignore needs for which resources are not available.

> We have treated the elderly where we have found them and provided them with traditional . . . services. The emphasis has been on helping them adjust to their station in life, rather than attempting to change their situation [Kosberg, 1976: 79].

In addition to working with larger systems in the society, an attempt to make the older client's environment more responsive includes work with others significant to the older client, including involved formal social systems, and informal systems such as family members and fictive kin. The necessity for involving these individuals in the service delivery process has been emphasized throughout this book. As those individuals who interact with the older client on a regular basis become involved in the service delivery process, they develop an investment in making responses to the older client in a manner that increases the client's ability to cope. The importance of matching the resources of these individuals to the needs of the elderly client should not be underestimated.

The families and friends of the elderly should not share in the service delivery process only because resources are limited, but should be involved because they are a viable resource for the older client. On the other hand, these individuals should not be expected to take over full responsibility for the elderly client when resources are limited (unless this is their wish as well as the desire of the older client), as this can violate their ability to be self-determining and has the potential to decrease the energy available to them. Utilizing a social systems perspective to analyze the situation of older clients and others significant to them will facilitate the service provider, client, and significant others as they seek to match resources to need in the most effective manner.

The service provider's involvement with those in the older client's immediate environment can also help in making larger, formal systems more responsive. Information about the informal situation of the older client can benefit the service provider in advocating for the older client and in educating policymakers. Only when the service provider has knowledge about the immediate environment of the older client can appropriate suggestions be made to those who determine how resources will be distributed. Nofz (1986: 86), in discussing the lack of resources available for rural elderly, asserts "that planning to provide for the needs of the rural elderly often suffers from inadequate knowledge of local conditions . . . and inability to take full advantage of existing support networks that lie outside the formal system of service delivery." This statement is true in planning to meet the needs of urban as well as of rural elderly.

Case management. Coordination of services for older clients should exist on both the individual and societal levels. Policies, such as the Older Americans Act, may mandate coordination of services for the elderly. However, unless coordination is a part of each program plan, services will not reflect the intent of the policy. Case management with elderly clients is not a new concept. As noted in Chapter 7, case management is beneficial to older clients regardless of the range of services available to them. However, as resources for elderly clients are depleted, case management is particularly necessary to ensure that services for older clients are effective and continuous.

Recently, several direct service providers described to me the negative effects that uncoordinated programs in their area had on older clients. In their county, two different agencies exist to provide services to abused elderly individuals. The two agencies have separate funding sources, but both have the responsibility of working with abused older clients. Although community members report incidents of abuse to both agencies, it has been agreed that one agency (Agency A) has the responsibility to turn its reports over to Agency B. Agency B, then, has agreed to investigate the cases and refer ongoing cases back to Agency A. However, if Agency B has too many abuse reports, Agency A will be asked to complete the investigation for them.

The service providers indicated that neither agency has assigned staff members who are responsible to follow clients and determine if reports have been acted on. As a result, service providers in both agencies occasionally receive calls, weeks after initial reports were made, questioning why the abuse was never investigated. In addition, clients referred back to Agency A for ongoing work may not be provided services if practitioners at that agency do not view the older client as being in immediate danger, even if professionals at Agency B reported that immediate danger exists. The benefits that case management would have in this situation are obvious. If one of the agencies had a case manager to whom all reports were given, that individual could follow though on each report, maintain an awareness of the status of each client, plan for and coordinate services indicated as necessary in the case notes, and evaluate the effectiveness of those services. As funding to agencies decreases and service providers have increased workloads, coordination of services between and within agencies is particularly important.

Case management can also provide for coordination of formal and informal services to older clients. For example, social workers in one long-term care facility coordinated the involvement of older residents, family members, and the nursing and the administrative staffs (Wells and Singer, 1985). Prior to the admission of an elderly resident, the social worker would visit the older person and his or her family in their home, providing them with information concerning the facility and returning to give information to nursing and administrative staff about the family and the potential resident. Following admission, social workers were responsible for continued communication between these individuals. In linking the social systems with whom the older client was involved and maintaining those linkages, the social workers facilitated exchanges of energy between all systems and helped to prevent misunderstandings and unfulfilled expectations.

Service providers carrying out case management tasks enhance their work by adhering to human service values and purposes and by gaining knowledge about the systems with which they interact. For example, the case manager who respects the dignity of all systems involved, and who attempts to maximize the self-determination of each system involved with the older client, is more likely to experience success than one who does not. In approaching the various individuals and agencies involved with a social systems perspective, the case manager increases the possibility of facilitating exchanges of energy that are beneficial to the older client as well as to others engaged in the service delivery process.

Education and research. The success of work with the elderly in the future will, to a large extent, depend on education of service providers and research about older clients. In discussing social work education, Kosberg (1976: 80) stresses, "Social work education should isolate and identify the elderly as a target population in need of greater social work attention and intervention." The need for gerontological education of undergraduate social work students has also been emphasized in the literature (T. Brubaker, 1985).

Individuals from various professions that provide services to the elderly have been found to hold stereotypic beliefs about the aged population (Keith, 1977; Troll and Scholsberg, 1970), including medical and social work students (Kosberg and Harris, 1978). Stereotypic beliefs about the elderly will prevent service providers from perceiving older clients and their situations as unique. When this occurs, as discussed in Chapter 5, service providers are unlikely to gain accurate information about older clients and the other individuals with whom they interact. Education can provide information that will enable the service provider to recognize that each older client is an individual. Education can also give practitioners knowledge about how to approach older clients and how to encourage elderly clients' environments to become more responsive to the clients' needs.

Education can take the form of in-service training to groups of practitioners as well as to students who are training for work in the human service field. Education about older clients can be conducted through direct provision of information, guided experiences with the elderly (E. Brubaker, 1985b), role plays (Greene, 1983), and through the use of other methods that provide information and the opportunity to apply that information through experiences with older clients.

Education of current and potential service providers is dependent on research about older clients. Research provides information for direct service providers. In addition to being consumers of research, service providers can be, and often are, contributors to research concerning the elderly. Practitioners contribute to journals such as *Social Casework, Social Work, Family Relations, Journal of Gerontological Social Work,* and *The Gerontologist.* Service providers have a responsibility to share information about elderly clients that will be helpful to other practitioners. The more that is known about the environment of elderly individuals and how resources can be successfully matched to needs, the more effective service providers will be in their work with older clients.

SUMMARY

Service providers working with elderly clients are likely to encounter increased caseloads as funding is decreased and as the older population expands. Providers of direct services have several avenues of response to this. Responses can include advocacy, working to make older client's environments more responsive to their needs, case management, and education and research. As service providers carry out these activities, they will experience more success when they apply values, purpose, and knowledge to tasks that are completed during the relationship with the client. Effectiveness is also increased by maintaining a social systems perspective and an awareness of the general and individual needs of elderly clients.

References

AIKEN, L. R. (1982) Later Life. New York: Holt, Rinehart & Winston.

ALVIREZ, D., F. D. BEAN, and D. WILLIAMS (1981) "The Mexican American family," in C. H. Mindel and R. W. Habenstein (eds.) Ethnic families in America: Patterns and variations. New York: Elsevier.

ANDERSON, R. E. and I. CARTER (1984) Human Behavior in the Social Environment. New York: Aldine.

ANDERSON, T. B. (1984) "Widowhood as a life transition: Its impact on kinship ties." Journal of Marriage and the Family 46: 105-113.

ATCHLEY, R. C. (1985) Social Forces and Aging. Belmont, CA: Wadsworth.

BALTES, P. B. and K. W. SCHAIE (1976) "On the plasticity of intelligence in adulthood and old age: Where Horn and Donaldson fail." American Psychologist 31: 720-725.

BARTLETT, H. M. (1970) The Common Base of Social Work Practice. New York: National Association of Social Workers.

BEAVER, M. L. (1983) Human Service Practice with the Elderly. Englewood Cliffs, NJ: Prentice-Hall.

BEAVER, M. L. and D. MILLER (1985) Clinical Social Work Practice with the Elderly. Homewood, IL: Dorsey Press.

BECVAR, R. J. and D. S. BECVAR (1982) Systems Theory and Family Therapy: A Primer. Washington, DC: University Press of America.

BERGER, R. M. and S. ANDERSON, (1984) "The in-home worker: Serving the frail elderly." Social Work 29: 456-461.

BERRIEN, F. K. (1968) General and Social Systems. New Brunswick, NJ: Rutgers University Press.

BILD, R. R. and R. J. HAVIGHURST (1976) "Senior citizens in great cities: The case of Chicago." The Gerontologist 16: 5-87.

BLAZER, D. G. (1982) Depression in Later Life. New York: C. V. Mosby.

BLENKNER, M. (1969) "The normal dependencies of aging," in R. Kalish (ed.) The Dependencies of Old People. Detroit: Institute of Gerontology, University of Michigan-Wayne State University.

BLENKNER, M. (1965) "Social work and family relationships in later life with some thoughts on filial maturity," in E. Shanas and G. Streib (eds.) Social Structure and the Family. Englewood Cliffs, NJ: Prentice-Hall.

BOOTH, R. (1983) "Toward an understanding of loneliness." Social Work 28: 116-119.

BOTWINICK, J. (1977) "Intellectual abilities," in J. E. Birren and K. W. Schaie (eds.) Handbook of the Psychology of Aging. New York: Van Nostrand Reinhold.

BOTWINICK, J. and M. STROANDT (1980) "Recall and recognition of old information in relation to age and sex." Journal of Gerontology 35: 70-76.

BRADSHAW, B. R., C. BRANDENBURG, J. BASHAM, and E. A. FERGUSON (1980) "Barriers to community-based long-term care." Journal of Gerontological Social Work 2: 185-198.

BRILL, N. I. (1985) Working with People: The Helping Process. New York: Longman.

BRODY, E. M. (1981) " 'Women in the middle' and family help to older people." The Gerontologist 21: 471-480.

BRODY, S., S. W. POULSHOCK, and C. F. MASCIOCCHI (1978) "The family caring unit: A major consideration in the long-term support system." The Gerontologist 18: 556-561.

BRUBAKER, E. (1983) "Providing services to older persons and their families," in T. H. Brubaker (ed.) Family Relationships in Later Life. Newbury Park, CA: Sage.

BRUBAKER, E. (1984) "Homemaker/home health aide supervisor's knowledge about older families." Caring 3: 44-47.

BRUBAKER, E. (1985a) "Older parents' reactions to the death of adult children: Implications for practice." Journal of Gerontological Social Work 9: 35-48.

BRUBAKER, E. (1985b) "Incorporating gerontological content into undergraduate social work curricula: Recommendations for the practice sequence." Gerontology and Geriatrics Education 5: 37-43.

BRUBAKER, E. and A. W. SCHIEFER (1987) "Groups with families of elderly long-term care residents: Building social support networks." Journal of Gerontological Social Work 10: 167-175.

BRUBAKER, T. H. (1985) Later Life Families. Newbury Park, CA.: Sage.

BRUBAKER, T. H. and E. BRUBAKER (1984) "Family support of older persons in the long-term care setting: Recommendations for practice," in W. H. Quinn and G. A. Hughston (eds.) Independent Aging: Family and Social Systems Perspectives. Rockville, MD: Aspen.

BRUBAKER, T. H. and E. BRUBAKER (1981) "Adult child and elderly parent households: Issues in stress for theory and practice." Alternative Lifestyles 4: 242-256.

BURNSIDE, I. (1984) Working with the Elderly: Group Process and Techniques. Belmont, CA: Wadsworth.

BUTLER R. N. and M. I. LEWIS (1982) Aging and Mental Health. St. Louis: C. V. Mosby.

CANTOR, M. H. (1975) "Life space and the social support system of inner city elderly of New York." The Gerontologist 15: 23-27.

CANTOR, M. H. and M. J. MAYER (1978) "Factors in differential utilization of services by urban elderly." Journal of Gerontological Social Work 1: 47-61.

CICIRELLI, V. (1983) "A comparison of helping behavior to elderly parents of adult children with intact and disrupted marriages." The Gerontologist 23: 619-625.

CICIRELLI, V. (1983) "Adult children and their elderly parents," in T. H. Brubaker (ed.) Family Relations in Later Life. Newbury Park, CA: Sage.

COMPTON, B. H. and B. GALAWAY (1979) Social Work Processes. Homewood, IL: Dorsey Press.

COMPTON, B. H. and B. GALAWAY (1983) Social Work Processes. Homewood, IL: Dorsey Press.

COOPER, S. (1977) "Social work: A dissenting profession." Social Work 22: 360-368.

DEAR, R. B. and R. J. PATTI (1981) "Legislative advocacy: Seven effective tactics." Social Work 26: 289-296.

DINITTO, D. M. and T. R. DYE (1983) Social Welfare: Politics and Public Policy. Englewood Cliffs, NJ: Prentice-Hall.

EDINBERG, M. A. (1985) Mental Health Practice with the Elderly. Englewood Cliffs, NJ: Prentice-Hall.

EISLER, T. A. (1984) "Career impact on independence of the elderly," in W. H. Quinn and G. A. Hughston (eds.) Independent Aging: Family and Social Systems Perspectives. Rockville, MD: Aspen.

EPSTEIN, L. (1980) Helping People: The Task Centered Approach. St. Louis: C. V. Mosby.

ERIKSON, E. (1963) Childhood and Society. New York: W. W. Norton.

FALLOTT, R. (1979-1980) "The impact on mood of verbal reminiscing in later adulthood." International Journal of Aging and Human Development 10: 385-400.

FEDERICO, R. C. (1983) The Social Welfare Institution: An Introduction. Lexington, MA: D. C. Heath.

FISCHER, J. (1978) Effective Casework Practice: An Eclectic Approach. New York: McGraw-Hill.

FOWLES, D. G. (1984) Profile of Older Americans: 1984. Washington, DC: American Association of Retired Persons. (pamphlet)

FRIEDMAN, S. R. and L. W. KAYE (1979) "Homecare for the frail elderly: Implications for an interactional relationship." Journal of Gerontological Social Work 2: 109-123.

GALLAGHER, D. E., L. W. THOMPSON, and J. A. PETERSON (1981-1982) "Psychosocial factors affecting adaptation to bereavement in the elderly." International Journal of Aging and Human Development 14: 79-95.

GAMBRILL, E. (1983) Casework: A Competency Based Approach. Englewood Cliffs, NJ: Prentice-Hall.

GARFINKEL, R. (1975) "The reluctant therapist." The Gerontologist 15: 136-137.

GELFAND, D. E. (1984) The Aging Network: Programs and Services. New York: Springer.

GERMAIN, C. (1973) "An ecological perspective in casework practice." Social Casework (June): 323-330.

GETZEL, G. (1983) "Group work with kin and friends caring for the elderly," in S. Saul (ed.) Group Work with the Frail Elderly. New York: Haworth Press.

GINSBURG, A. B. and S. G. GOLDSTEIN (1974) "Age bias in referral for psychological consultation." Journal of Gerontology 29: 410-415.

GOLAN, N. (1986) "Crisis theory," in F. J. Turner (ed.) Social Work Treatment: Interlocking Theoretical Approaches. New York: Free Press.

GORDON, W. E. (1969) "Basic constructs for an integrative and generative conception of social work," in G. A. Hearn (ed.) The General Systems Approach: Contributions Toward an Holistic Conception of Social Work. New York: Council on Social Work Education.

GOULDNER, A. W. (1960) "The norm of reciprocity: A preliminary statement." American Sociological Review 25 (April): 161-178.

GREENE, V. L. and D. J. MONAHAN (1982) "The impact of visitation on patient well-being in nursing homes." The Gerontologist 22: 418-423.

GROSS-ANDREW, S. and A. H. ZIMMER (1978) "Incentives to families caring for disabled elderly: Research and demonstration project to strengthen the natural supports systems." Journal of Gerontological Social Work 1: 119-133.

HARBERT, A. S. and L. S. GINSBERG (1979) Human Services for Older Adults: Concepts and Skills. Belmont, CA: Wadsworth.

HARTMAN, A. (1981) "The family: A central focus for practice." Social Work 26: 7-13.

HEPWORTH, D. H. and J. A. LARSEN (1986) Direct Social Work Practice: Theory and Skills. Chicago, IL: Dorsey Press.

HERR, J. J. and J. H. WEAKLAND (1979) Counseling Elders and Their Families. New York: Springer.

HESS, B. P. and J. M. WARING (1978) "Changing patterns of aging and family bonds in later life." The Family Coordinator 27: 303-314.

HESS, B. P. and E. W. MARKSON (1980) Aging and Old Age. New York: Macmillan.

HOOK, W. F., J. SOBAL, and J. C. OAK (1982) "Frequency of visitation in nursing homes: Patterns of contact across the boundaries of total institutions." The Gerontologist 22: 424-428.

HORN, J. L. and G. DONALDSON (1976) "On the myth of intellectual decline in adulthood." American Psychologist 31: 701-719.

HOROWITZ, A. and SHINDELMAN, L. (1983) "Reciprocity and affection: Past influences on current caregiving." Journal of Gerontological Social Work 5: 5-19.

INGERSOLL, B. and L. GOODMAN (1980) "History comes alive: Facilitating reminiscence in a group of institutionalized elderly." Journal of Gerontological Social Work 2(4): 305-319.

JACK, S. and P. RIES (1981) "Current estimates from the national health interview survey: United States 1979." Data from the National Health Interview Survey, Series 10(136). Rockville, Maryland: NCHS.

JANZEN, O. and C. HARRIS (1980) Family Treatment in Social Work Practice. Itasca, IL: F. E. Peacock.

JANZEN, O. and C. HARRIS (1986) Family Treatment in Social Work Practice. Itasca, IL: F. E. Peacock.

JOHNSON, E. S. (1978) " 'Good' relationships between older mothers and their daughters: A causal model." The Gerontologist 18: 301-306.

KAMERMAN, S. B. and A. J. KAHN (1976) Social Services in the United States: Policies and Programs. Philadelphia: Temple University Press.

KAUFMAN, A. (1980) "Social policy and long-term care of the aged." Social Work 25: 133-137.

KAY, D.W.K. and K. BERGMANN (1980) "Epidemiology of mental disorders among the aged in the community," in J. E. Birren and R. B. Sloane (eds.) Handbook of Mental Health and Aging. Englewood Cliffs, NJ: Prentice-Hall.

KEEFE, T. and D. E. MAYPOLE (1983) Relationships in Social Service Practice: Context and Skills. Monterey, CA: Brooks/Cole.

KIRSCHNER, C. (1979) "The aging family in crisis: A problem in living." Social Casework 60: 209-216.

KOHEN, J. A. (1983) "Old but not alone: Informal supports among the elderly by marital status and sex." The Gerontologist 23: 57-63.

KONOPKA, G. (1983) Social Group Work: A Helping Process. Englewood Cliffs, NJ: Prentice-Hall.

KOSBERG, J. I. (1976) "A social problems approach to gerontology in social work eduction." Journal of Education for Social Work 12: 78-84.

KOSBERG, J. I. and A. P. HARRIS (1978) "Attitudes toward elderly clients." Health and Social Work 3: 67-90.

LAWSON, G. and B. HUGHES (1980) "Some considerations for the training of counselors who work with the elderly." Counseling and Values (3): 204-208.

LEBOWITZ, B. D. (1978) "Old age and family functioning." Journal of Gerontological Social Work 1: 111-118.

LOWY, L. (1983) "Social group work with vulnerable older persons: Theoretical perspective," in S. Saul (ed.) Group Work with the Frail Elderly. New York: Haworth Press.

LOWY, L. (1985) Social Work with the Aging. Second Edition. New York: Harper & Row.

MALUCCIO, A. N. and W. D. MARLOW (1984) "The Case for the Contract," in B. Compton and B. Galaway (eds.) Social Work Processes. Third Edition. Homewood, IL: Dorsey Press.

MAYER, M. J. (1983) "Demographic change and the elderly population," in S. Saul (ed.) Group Work with the Frail Elderly. New York: Haworth Press.

McCLUSKY, H. E. (1973) "Education for aging: The scope and the field and perspective for the future," in S. N. Grabowski and M. W. Dean (eds.) Learning for Aging. Washington, DC: Adult Education Association.

McKINLAY, J. B. (1973) "Social networks, lay consultation and help-seeking behavior." Social Forces 51: 275-292.

MILLER, D. A. (1981) "The 'sandwich' generation: Adult children of the aged." Social Work 26: 419-423.

MINDEL, C. H. (1983) "The elderly in minority families," in T. H. Brubaker (ed.) Family Relationships in Later Life. Newbury Park, CA: Sage.

MINAHAN, A. and A. PINCUS (1977) "Conceptual framework for social work practice." Social Work 22: 347-352.

MONK, A. (1981) "Social work with the aged: Principles of practice." Social Work 26: 61-68.

NEUGARTEN, B. L. (1964) "A developmental view of adult personality," in J. E. Birren (ed.) Relations and Development of Aging. Springfield, IL: Charles C Thomas.

NOFZ, M. P. (1986) "Social services for older rural Americans: Some policy concerns." Social Work 31: 85-91.

O'BRIEN, J. E. and D. L. WAGNER (1980) "Help seeking by the frail elderly: Problems in network analysis." The Gerontologist 20(1): 78-83.

OKUN, B. F. (1982) Effective Helping: Interviewing and Counseling Techniques. Monterey, CA: Brooks/Cole.

OKUN, B. F. (1984) Working with Adults: Individual, Family, and Career Development. Monterey, CA: Brooks/Cole.

PINCUS, A. and A. MINAHAN (1973) Social Work Practice: Model and Method. Itasca, IL: F. E. Peacock Publishers.

PINKSTON, E. M. and N. L. LINSK (1984) Care of the Elderly: A Family Approach. New York: Pergamon Press.

REECE, D., T. WALZ, and H. HAGEBOEK (1983) "Intergenerational care providers of non-institutionalized frail elderly: Characteristics and consequences." Journal of Gerontology 5: 21-32.

REID, W. J. (1977) "Social work for social problems." Social Work 22: 374-381.

RILEY, M. W. and A. FONER (1968) Aging and Society. Volume I: An Inventory of Research Findings. New York: Russell Sage Foundation.

ROBINSON, B. and M. THURNER (1979) "Taking care of aged parents: A family cycle transition." The Gerontologist 19: 586-593.

ROBINSON, B. C. (1983) "Characteristics of the housebound elderly." The Gerontologist 23: 97.

SALZBERGER, R. (1979) "Casework and the client's right to self-determination." Social Work 24: 398-400.

SANDERS, G. F., J. WALTERS, and J. MONTGOMERY (1984) "Married elderly and their families." Family Perspective 18: 45-56.

SARGENT, S. S. [ed.] (1980) Nontraditional Therapy and Counseling with the Aging. New York: Springer.

SCHONFIELD, A.E.D. (1980) "Learning, memory and aging," in J. E. Birren and R. B. Sloane (eds.) Handbook of Mental Health and Aging. Englewood Cliffs, NJ: Prentice-Hall.

SCOTT, J. P. and V. R. KIVETT (1980) "The widowed, black, older adult in the rural south: Implications for policy." Family Relations 29: 83-90.

SEELBACH, W. C. (1984) "Filial responsibility and the care of aging family members," in W. H. Quinn and G. A. Hughston (eds.) Independent Aging: Family and Social Systems Perspective. Rockville, MD: Aspen.

SEELBACH, W. C. and W. J. SAUER (1977) "Filial responsibility expectations and realizations." Family Coordinator 27(4): 341-350.

SHANAS, E. (1979a) "Social myth as hypothesis: The case of the family relations of old people." The Gerontologist 19(1): 3-9.

SHANAS, E. (1979b) "The family as a social support system in age." The Gerontologist 19: 164-174.

SHANAS, E. (1968) "Family help patterns and social class in three countries." Journal of Marrige and the Family 29: 257-266.

SILVERSTONE, B. and A. BURACK-WEISS (1983) "The social work function in nursing homes and home care," in G. S. Getzel and M. J. Mellor (eds.) Gerontological Social Work Practice in Long-Term Care. New York: Haworth Press.

SIMOS, B. G. (1975) "Adult children and their aging parents," in C. H. Meyer (ed.) Social Work with the Aging. Washington, DC: National Association of Social Workers, Inc.

SKINNER, B. F. (1983) "Intellectual self-management in old age." American Psychologist 38: 239-245.

SOLOMON, R. (1983) "Serving families of the institutionalized aged: The four crises," in G. S. Getzel and M. J. Mellor (eds.) Gerontological Social Work Practice in Long-Term Care. New York: Haworth Press.

SPRINGER, D. and T. H. BRUBAKER (1984) Family Caregivers and Dependent Elderly. Newbury Park, CA: Sage.

STEINBERG, R. M. and G. W. CARTER (1983) Case Management and the Elderly. Lexington, MA: Lexington Books.

STEINMETZ, S. K. and D. J. AMSDEN (1983) "Dependent elders, family stress and abuse," in T. H. Brubaker (ed.) Family Relationships in Later Life. Newbury Park, CA: Sage.

STEHOUWER, J. (1965) "Relations between generations and three generation household in Denmark," in E. Shanas and G. F. Streib (eds.) Social Structure and the Family. Englewood Cliffs, NJ: Prentice-Hall.

STEINMAN, L. (1979) "Reactivated conflicts with an aging parent," in R. K. Ragan (ed.) Aging Parents. Los Angeles: University of Southern California Press.

STREIB, G. F. (1972) "Older families and their troubles: Familial and social responses." Family Coordinator 21: 5-19.

STREIB, G. F. and M. A. HILKER (1980) "The cooperative family: An alternative lifestyle for the elderly." Alternative Lifestyles 3: 167-184.

STROLLER, E. P. (1983) "Parental caregiving by adult children." Journal of Marriage and the Family: 851-858.

SUSSMAN, M. B. (1977) "Family bureaucracy and the elderly individual: An organizational/linkage perspective," in E. Shanas and M. B. Sussman (eds.) Family, Bureaucracy and the Elderly. Durham, NC: Duke University Press.

TAUBMAN, S. (1985) "Doing less with less." Social Work 30: 180-182.

UNGER, D. G. and D. R. POWELL (1980) "Supporting families under stress: The role of social networks." Family Relations 29: 566-574.

WAKE, S. B. and J. SPORAKOWSKI (1972) "An intergenerational comparison of attitudes toward supporting parents." Journal of Marriage and the Family 34: 42-48.

WANTZ, M. and J. GAY (1981) The aging process: A health perspective. Cambridge, MA: Winthrop Publishers.

WEEKS, J. R. (1984) Aging: Concepts and Social Issues. Belmont, CA: Wadsworth.

WEINER, M. B., A. J. BROK, and A. M. SANDOWSKY (1978) Working with the Aged. Englewood Cliffs, NJ: Prentice-Hall.

WELLS, L. M. and C. SINGER (1985) "A model for linking networks in social work practice with the institutionalized elderly." Social Work 30: 318-322.

WIGDOR, B. T. (1980) "Drives and motivations with aging," in J. E. Birren and R. B. Sloane (eds.) Handbook of Mental Health and Aging. Englewood Cliffs, NJ: Prentice-Hall.

WILSON, S. J. (1978) Confidentiality in Social Work: Issues and Principles. New York: Free Press.

"Working Definition of Social Work Practice." (1958) As reprinted in Social Work 22: 44.

"Working Statement on the Purpose of Social Work." (1981) Social Work 26:6.

ZARIT, S. H., K. E. REEVER, and J. BACH-PETERSON (1980) "Relatives of the impaired elderly: Correlates of feelings of burden.'' The Gerontologist 20: 649-655.

ZASTROW, C. (1985) The Practice of Social Work. Homewood, IL: Dorsey Press.

Index

About the Author

ELLIE BRUBAKER is an Associate Professor in the Department of Sociology and Anthropology at Miami University, Oxford, Ohio. She completed a Ph.D. in social work at the Ohio State University and received an M.S.W. from the University of Iowa. She is a member of the Academy of Certified Social Workers. Her research has been published in a number of journals, such as *Journal of Gerontological Social Work, American Behavioral Scientist, Gerontology and Geriatrics Education,* as well as other scholarly journals. In addition, she has authored several chapters in edited volumes focusing on older families. Her research has focused on social service delivery to older clients and their families. Her experience includes social work with elderly clients, and she consults with social service programs directed toward older individuals.